D1605069

First Bites

First Bites

HOMEMADE, NOURISHING RECIPES FROM BABY SPOONFULS TO TODDLER TREATS

LEIGH ANN CHATAGNIER

Skyhorse Publishing

Visit our website at www.skyhorsepublishing.com.

10 9 8 7 6 5 4 3 2 1

Library of Congress Cataloging-in-Publication Data is available on file.

Cover design by Jenny Zemanek
Cover photograph by Leigh Ann Chatagnier

Print ISBN: 978-1-5107-2401-3
Ebook ISBN: 978-1-5107-2403-7

Printed in China

To the most delicious thing I've ever had a hand in creating, my son Parks. Thank you for making me a mommy and opening up my heart to a whole new kind of love. My hope for you is that your appetite for life will stay as big as your appetite for all the delicious things you will taste. Love well, eat well, and go after all the things your heart desires—because life is short and these are the things that matter. I love you as big as the beach always and forever! XX

Contents

Introduction

When I became pregnant with my son Parks, I knew I would be making all his food, no question. The thought of tantalizing his tiny taste buds with new flavors and textures made me so excited! I couldn't wait to share my love of real food with him. Instilling healthy eating habits from an early age has always been a top priority to me and with that, I also wanted his food to be packed full of flavor. After all, why should baby food be lacking in the taste department? They want to eat yummy things too!

I couldn't wait until Parks was finally old enough to start introducing him to solids, and I do mean that I counted down the days . . . I have always had so much fun creating flavor combinations with foods that I know are good for his rapidly growing body *and* that he loves also—his little *mmm*s are music to my ears!

I am a food enthusiast through and through. I have always loved being in the kitchen, and cooking for my family is something that brings me so much joy. When my guys clean their plates, I get the utmost satisfaction of not only knowing that their food tasted great, but also that it was really good for them too.

My husband and I have always eaten "real food," and by that I mean non-processed ingredients that are preferably sourced locally when possible. I think it's important that babies get the chance to eat this way too, and to me, making their food from scratch is the only way to truly do that. From a cost perspective, all the way to simply knowing the ingredients your child is eating, there are a multitude of reasons why homemade is the way to go.

Getting your baby involved in the process of cooking from the start, even if that only means he or she is beating on pots and pans on the floor, gives your child a better opportunity to appreciate what they are eating later in life! When kids help prepare the food they eat, they are more likely to make good choices for themselves. I grew up in the kitchen with my mom making healthy food, and nothing would give me greater joy than if my son enjoys being in the kitchen making delicious food as much as I do.

As a mom, I am a realist, and there is always a battle with time to get things accomplished. Planning and preparation is a huge part of making homemade baby food, but it can be done! There are going to be days when you just aren't going to have the time to make a meal from scratch. That's why in this book you will find recipes that you can make ahead and will freeze beautifully. Meal prepping in advance ensures that your little one has something nutritious and homemade to eat more times than not.

When life gets busy, mamas tend to put themselves on the back burner—which is why I have also included a chapter of my favorite recipes just for moms. I eat these on a regular basis to keep my energy high, and they also keep me from snacking unhealthily when I don't have time for a sit-down meal! After all, mommies and daddies need to take care of themselves too in order for us to be our best selves for our kids.

In this book, I will show you how to take your baby on a journey of learning to love food (healthy food) right from the start! From the first bite they taste, up until they are at the dinner table eating homemade meals that were prepared for the whole family, my hope is that you will end up with a toddler who has a seasoned palate for good, healthy food. It is going to be so fun for you to watch your baby's eyes light up with delight when they taste something delicious that you made for them with love! There is such satisfaction in knowing that your hard work is 100 percent worth it.

My goal for you is that you will feel confident about the food you are making for your babies. I can only hope that you will find the joy I have in knowing you are nurturing the growth of a beautiful little human who truly needs nutritious, real food to keep up with their growing bodies. It's going to be so exciting when you end up with a little foodie who appreciates cooking and eating just as much as you do!

Getting Started

Organic vs. Non-Organic

Which to Buy for What

With so much hype about why to buy organic food, it can be overwhelming to decide when to buy organic and when not to. With use of pesticides and chemicals being at an all-time high, organic tends to be the best option. I will be the first to admit that it can get a little costly at times, which can be a drawback for a lot of parents, including me. After all, one of the perks to making your own baby food is to save money, right? But even with organic food costing a little bit more, I have found that in most cases, it is still less expensive in the long run than buying already-prepared baby food. For instance, you can get 4–6 servings of baby food out of one single sweet potato! That's incredibly cost effective if you break it down that way.

Even if you decide that you can't swing buying organic all the time or at all, you are still doing amazing things for your baby! By giving them such a great start at being healthy and making them homemade food from fresh ingredients, you are exposing them to real food at an early age. This alone will in turn make them healthier children, teenagers, and adults. You are shaping them into healthy individuals who will be aware of what they are putting into their bodies, and that is something to be extremely proud of!

Certain foods contain higher levels of contaminants than others, and there is a list released every year naming the top produce items that are recommended to buy organic to avoid those chemicals. There is also a list of produce that is safe in its non-organic version because they haven't been altered with as many contaminants.

Here's a list of the "dirty dozen" vegetables and fruits that are recommended to buy organic, and the top twelve vegetables and fruits that are least contaminated, per the most recent information.

Dirty Dozen
(produce you should buy organic)

Peaches
Apples
Bell Peppers
Celery
Nectarines
Strawberries
Cherries
Pears
Grapes (Imported)
Spinach
Lettuce
Potatoes

Twelve Least Contaminated
(produce that doesn't always need to be organic)

Onions
Avocado
Sweet Corn (Frozen)
Pineapples
Mango
Asparagus
Sweet Peas (Frozen)
Kiwi Fruit
Bananas
Cabbage
Broccoli
Papaya

As far as meat, dairy, and eggs go, I usually always buy organic when I can (if I can get it from a local farm, even better!). I am by no means an expert, just a mom who cares about the ingredients I am feeding my family, just like you.

One of my favorite ways to save money is by visiting my local farmers' market. There, you can see where your food is coming from and they will tell you whether or not their product is organic. It's usually a more cost-effective way of shopping, as the prices are typically less than the organic produce in your local supermarket.

Another favorite trick is to buy bulk when organic produce is on sale in your grocery store, because you can always freeze it for later use! I will buy five or six pints of berries if they are on sale and freeze them in bags for smoothies, purees, etc. Same goes for organic meat! Always keep your eyes peeled for deals.

Allergies

What Are Foods That You Should Be Cautious of and What Are the Signs?

If you or your family have a history of any certain allergy, it is definitely smart to be extra cautious with that ingredient for your baby. If there is no family history, it's much less likely your baby will have a food allergy. However, there are still cases of that not being true, which is why I always say to make sure you wait a few days after introducing a new food to your baby before introducing another new ingredient. You also want to try and introduce it early in the day in case of a reaction, that way you aren't dealing with a sick babe in the middle of the night!

The old rule for introducing foods like eggs, peanuts, and shellfish used to be to wait until the child was over a year old. However, recent studies have said that introducing these foods at an earlier age (as early as six months) can actually help prevent the child from developing an allergy, particularly with peanuts. This is something that you will want to research for yourself and discuss with your child's pediatrician before you decide to go forward with any of these potentially allergy-related ingredients.

Per the approval of his pediatrician, I did introduce peanut butter around seven months to my son, as well as letting him have a whole egg (instead of just the yolk, which is sometimes recommended since the allergic reaction usually occurs due to the whites of an egg) with no problems. You obviously have to decide for yourself what you feel comfortable doing as a mom, and always talk to your child's pediatrician about what he or she recommends as well!

Foods to be Extra Cautious With:
Cow's Milk
Wheat or Gluten
Citrus
Shellfish
Peanuts or any Tree Nut

> **Note:** Symptoms that your baby is allergic to a certain food may include stomach pains, diarrhea, or skin rashes. These symptoms sometimes show up immediately, but can take a day or two to appear. Always make sure you talk to your child's pediatrician if you think he or she has an allergy.

Foods to Avoid Until Twelve Months of Age or Older

Cow's Milk: It should not be introduced until after one year because babies need breast milk or formula to ensure they are getting the nutrients they need. Cow's milk does not contain enough iron and other essential vitamins that a baby younger than twelve months needs and can be harder to digest for them.

Citrus: This one can be tricky as some babies do not have a reaction to it, while other have a sensitivity to the high acidic content. Use your best judgment on whether your baby is ready and will like it or not. (My son will eat a lemon without puckering no problem, every child is different.)

Fresh Berries: This is another instance to use your best judgment as berries also have a high acidic content and some babies show a sensitivity to them. If cooked, berries usually will be easier on a baby's tummy. Note: If you are giving blueberries to a baby, make sure to cut them in half until they are ready to eat one whole without choking, usually until they are twelve months old.

Grapes: Grapes can be a serious choking hazard. Even after your child is twelve months old, it is recommended to cut grapes in half lengthwise to prevent choking.

When introducing any of these foods, makes sure you consider your family history and your child's track record on introducing new foods.

Honey: Honey can cause botulism in an infant due to their immature tummies until after they reach one year of age. Try using maple syrup as a natural sweetener instead.

Proper Food Storage

How to Store in the Refrigerator and Freezer

Purees: Most purees can be stored in the fridge for two to three days before freezing. Store leftover purees in BPA-free baby food trays similar to ice cube trays. Most of them come with tops to prevent freezer burn and will stay good for up to a month.

Other Food: For most recipes in this book, you can store the leftover baby food in individual BPA-free containers in the fridge for two to three days or in the freezer for up to a month.

Note: bananas and avocados are two foods that do not store well and should be eaten the same day.

Why BPA free?

BPA stands for bisphenol A, a chemical used to make plastics. It has been linked to certain side effects that can be detrimental to your health, and particularly for infants. There are always studies going on, so to be safe I always recommend BPA-free storage containers.

Dairy Guidelines

When to Introduce Cheeses and Yogurts?

While you will want to wait to introduce cow's milk to your baby until after he or she is one year of age, you can introduce yogurts and cheeses at an earlier age of anywhere between six and eight months! Talk to your child's pediatrician about what is best for your baby, but we decided to introduce yogurts, hard cheeses, and cottage cheese around seven months for my son. They are great sources of protein and I like to make sure I buy the yogurt that has live cultures in it for a good dose of probiotics too! I also check that I get plain whole-milk Greek or regular yogurt so that there is no sugar added. You can top it with fresh fruit or any of your child's favorite purees to balance the tartness of the yogurt so they are only getting the natural fruit sugars.

If your baby has a dairy sensitivity, try out a soy-based yogurt or coconut yogurt instead.

Healthy Fats for Your Baby

Your baby needs extra fat for their rapidly growing bodies as well as their brains and nervous systems.

My favorite healthy fats for a baby's diet include:

Coconut oil
Olive oil
Avocado oil
Full-fat coconut milk
Avocados
Chia seeds

These healthy fats can be found throughout this book in smoothies, to use for roasting, etc., making it easy to incorporate them into your child's diet.

Probiotics for Babies

Probiotics are fantastic for babies and toddlers of all ages. It gives their tummies a good dose of healthy bacteria that helps with their digestion and immune system, especially once they start on solid foods specifically, as their gut will completely change. Probiotics have also been known to help clear up eczema and are especially important if your child is on antibiotics, to keep their tummies happy. One of the best ways to ensure your child is getting probiotics is to incorporate foods into their diet such as yogurts and kefir. (Just make sure you are looking at the ingredients to check that it contains live cultures.)

You can also give your baby a probiotic supplement that your child's pediatrician can recommend for you. As with anything else, always discuss with your child's pediatrician before starting anything new with their diet!

The Basics

Get Started Making Homemade Baby Food

Honestly, you don't need a whole lot to get started making homemade food in your own kitchen. You can get by with basic kitchen equipment. Here are some necessities:

- High-powered blender or food processor (a food processor will not puree food as smoothly as a high-powered blender can)
- BPA-free storage containers with lids
- BPA-free ice cube trays with lids
- Sharp paring knives
- Cutting boards
- Saucepans
- Baking sheets
- Skillet
- Wooden spoons
- Baby spoons
- Electric hand mixer or stand mixer
- Steamer basket
- Baby bowls and plates

How do you know if your baby is ready for solid food?

The biggest question when your baby is getting ready to enter the phase of eating solid food is, "How do I know when my baby is ready?" Every baby is different, but most pediatricians will recommend starting solids anywhere between four and six months of age.

Factors that let you know that your baby is ready other than age include:
- Baby can hold their head and neck up without support.
- Baby shows interest in other people eating food.
- Baby consumes more than thirty-two ounces of milk in a day.
- Baby leans toward a spoon as if he or she wants to eat from it.
- Baby seems dissatisfied from milk alone.

As always, if you think your baby is ready, talk to your pediatrician if you have any hesitations.

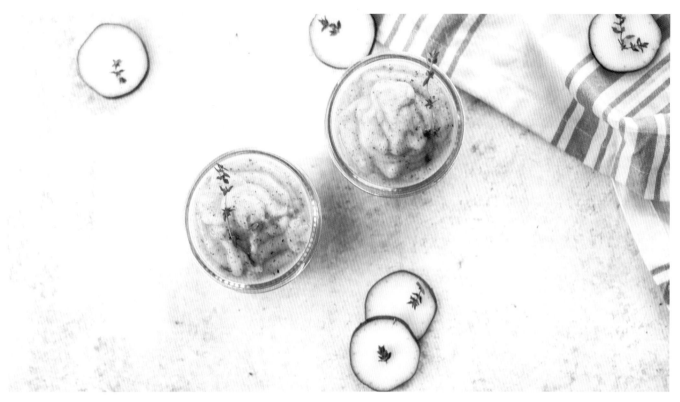

Pantry and Refrigerator Staples

All-purpose flour
Almond milk
Avocado oil
Baking powder
Baking soda
Black beans, canned
Black pepper
Bread crumbs
Brown rice
Chia seeds
Chicken broth (low-sodium)
Chickpeas, canned
Cinnamon
Coconut milk
Coconut oil
Cow's milk
Curry powder
Eggs
Flaxseed
Frozen fruit (for smoothies especially)
Frozen vegetables (peas, broccoli, spinach, corn)
Garlic powder
Hemp seeds
Honey
Kefir
Lentils
Maple syrup
Olive oil
Pinto beans, canned
Plain whole-milk yogurt
Pumpkin, canned
Rolled oats
Salt
Steel-cut oats
Unsweetened applesauce (if you prefer not making your own)
Variety of fresh fruit
White beans, canned
Whole wheat flour
Whole wheat pasta
Wild caught salmon, canned
Wild caught tuna, canned

Favorite Finger Foods

Avocado pieces
Banana pieces
Black beans
Broccoli florets
Cheerios (just the plain ones with no additional sugar added)
Cheese
Cooked butternut squash cubes
Cooked sweet potato cubes
Crackers
Scrambled eggs
Sliced blueberries
Soft fruit (peeled peaches and pears)

Little Spoonfuls

6+ months

Starting Your Baby on Solids

Starting your little one on solids is such a fun and exciting time! Experimenting with new flavors your baby will love can give you great satisfaction as a parent. You will be surprised at how your baby embraces vegetables, fruits, and spices of all varieties and you can feel great knowing they are getting nutrient-packed little spoonfuls of yumminess.

This stage is my favorite because most babies are not picky and are very excited about tasting new flavors! While it might take them a few tries to figure out the whole swallowing-solid-foods thing, as well as what these new textures are in their mouths, I can promise they will get the hang of it in no time!

I always tell other parents who hesitate or are nervous about starting solid foods to begin simple. My favorite foods to introduce at the beginning are avocado, banana, and sweet potato, as these have the least possibility of an allergic reaction. It is best to always wait a couple of days before introducing a new food or spice to your little one, especially at the beginning, to ensure their bodies are digesting the ingredient correctly and to make sure that they do not have any sort of reaction to the food introduced. If all seems good after two days or so, you can move on to the next introduction.

Some other ideas for the early stages of fruits or vegetables include, but are not limited to, green beans, pears, apples, zucchini, and squash. All these foods have very little chance for a reaction from your baby. Once you feel your child is ready for a little bit of extra flavor, you can start with a little cinnamon in some fruit or a sweet potato. From there, you can try adding a bit of cumin, curry powder, chili powder, black pepper, or garlic powder to other purees. You, always want to start with a tiny amount of any spice, of course—an eighth of a teaspoon or less at the beginning.

Always follow the wait-and-watch method before trying out something new.

Every baby is different and some will like spices more than others! In my experience, my son has always appreciated extra flavor in his food. The more you introduce to them the better, as it will expand their tiny palates and make them better eaters later on in their toddler years when they begin to have an opinion on what they are eating (and believe me, they will get an opinion!).

Another tip I always tell mamas is that even if your baby turns their nose up to something one day, try it again in a week or so and I bet they will change their mind! Don't give up after one try, sometimes it takes a couple of introductions before their taste buds get used to it and decide they like it. Whatever you do, don't get discouraged—this time is all about trial and error, and you are doing a great job!

Finding time to make your own baby food can seem daunting at times, but I will tell you what works for me. I like to pick one day a week where I can carve out a couple of hours to prep the food. I chop, steam, roast, and puree my heart out and try to get as much made as I can in the allotted time (usually nap time). From there, I keep a couple portions in the refrigerator and then freeze what's left to ensure there are always a few options for food that are ready to pop out and thaw whenever I need it for any meal.

I have combined some of my favorite puree combos that your baby is going to love trying out. I still make a few of these purees today and add them into pancakes, waffles, and make my own squeezable pouches now that my son is older. Even if you are strictly doing baby-led weaning (which is where you skip purees and go strictly to letting baby learn to feed themselves with finger foods), you may still want to use a few of these purees for other recipes.

Watch your baby learn to love food with wholesome and delicious recipes right from the beginning!

Recipes

Note: *All purees make 8–12 one-ounce servings.*

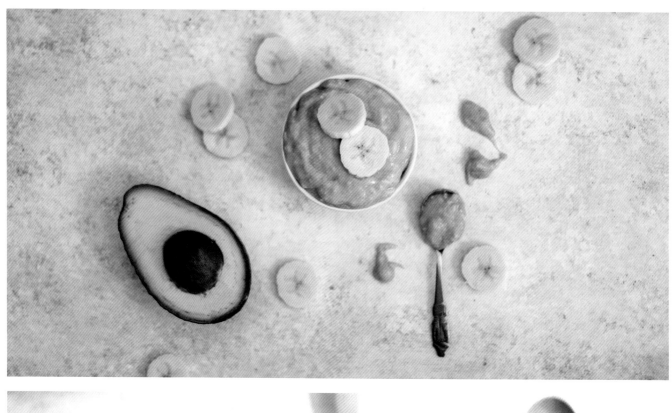

Avocado Banana Smash

This creamy puree will be a sure favorite of your little one and is a great first combination for beginners to try out, with only two ingredients! What's even better than how much your baby will love this recipe is that you don't even need a food processor to get it to the perfect consistency!

Ingredients

½ avocado, peeled

1 ripe banana

Directions

1. Mash together avocado and banana with a fork until smooth.
2. Serve immediately.

Note: This recipe does not refrigerate or freeze well and should be eaten within the hour it is prepared.

Persimmon Cantaloupe Puree

This puree requires no prep other than peeling the fruit and placing it into a blender! Cantaloupe is high in vitamins C and A and is so nutritious for your little one.

Ingredients

1 ripe persimmon,
 skin removed

1 cup ripe cantaloupe,
 peeled and seeded

Directions

1. Place ingredients into the blender and process until smooth.
2. Serve immediately or store in the refrigerator or freezer for a later date.

Curried Coconut Sweet Potatoes

These sweet potatoes get a flavor burst from the curry powder, and the addition of coconut milk provides healthy fats your baby needs for his or her rapidly growing body! Watch your little one's face light up when they taste a spoonful of this creamy puree.

Ingredients

2 large sweet potatoes
   (about 2 cups)
1 tsp. curry powder
¼–½ cup full-fat
   coconut milk

Directions

1. Preheat oven to 450 degrees.

2. Wash sweet potatoes and dry thoroughly. Poke holes over the entire sweet potato with a fork or knife to prevent exploding in the oven.

3. Roast potatoes on an aluminum foil-lined baking sheet for about an hour, until they are tender.

4. Let the potatoes cool slightly, then remove the peel.

5. Place potatoes into a food processor or blender with the curry powder and coconut milk. Blend until smooth.

6. Serve immediately or store in the refrigerator or freezer for a later date.

Basil Green Beans

Adding fresh herbs to your baby's puree is a great way to introduce their taste buds to new flavors! Basil pairs perfectly with green beans here to create a fresh and delicious puree that will have your baby gobbling up every bite.

Ingredients

1 cup fresh green beans, ends removed
1 small garlic clove, smashed and peeled (optional)
¼ tsp. black pepper
1 cup water
1 tbsp. fresh basil, chopped

Directions

1. Add green beans, garlic, black pepper, and water to a medium saucepan and bring to a boil.
2. Reduce heat and simmer for 10–15 minutes, or until tender. Drain the beans, reserving some of the cooking water.
3. Add green beans, garlic clove, and basil leaves to a blender, along with a little of the water the green beans were boiled in. Process until smooth. (If you are worried about the garlic being too strong for your baby, simply remove it from the water before processing so that there is only a mild garlic flavor.)
4. Add more liquid if necessary for consistency.
5. Serve immediately or store in the refrigerator or freezer for a later date.

Chunky Corn and Squash with Turmeric

Talk about a delicious and healthy puree for your little one! This combination, with the addition of turmeric, is sure to delight your baby's taste buds! Turmeric is an anti-inflammatory and is perfect to help aid in any teething issues your baby might be having.

Ingredients

1 tbsp. olive oil

2 yellow squash

½ cup fresh or frozen corn kernels

¼ tsp. turmeric powder

⅛ tsp. black pepper

Directions

1. Heat olive oil in a large skillet over medium heat.

2. Chop squash into 1-inch cubes and place in the skillet along with the corn, turmeric, and black pepper.

3. Sauté for 2–3 minutes and then place the lid on the skillet and let the squash and corn continue to cook until tender, about 15 minutes.

4. Place all ingredients into a food processor or blender and blend until slightly chunky.

5. Serve immediately or store in the refrigerator or freezer for a later date.

Peas with Kiwi, Apple, and Spinach

This puree is vibrant green, letting you know that it is full of essential vitamins every baby needs. Popeye would be proud of this spinach-packed puree, and you should be too!

Ingredients

1 cup frozen or fresh peas
½ cup fresh spinach
½ cup apple, peeled and diced
1 kiwi, peeled
1 tsp. lemon juice

Directions

1. Boil peas in a medium saucepan until tender, about 10 minutes, adding the spinach at the very end to wilt it slightly. Strain the liquid out, reserving some for the puree.

2. Soften the apples by steaming them or sautéing until tender.

3. Add all ingredients to a food processor and blend until smooth.

4. Add in some of the liquid from the peas if needed for consistency.

5. Serve immediately, or store in the refrigerator or freezer for a later date.

Beet Applesauce

Beets are an earthy superfood containing a high content of vitamins, and when mixed with apples they become sweet and delicious! Your baby is going to love this vibrant new take on applesauce!

Ingredients

1 cup beet, peeled and chopped (about 1 large beet)

1 cup apple, peeled and cored

1 tsp. cinnamon

⅛ tsp. ground clove

Directions

1. Chop the beet into 1-inch pieces and place into a steamer basket. Steam the beet for 45 minutes.

2. For the last 15 minutes, add the diced apple to the beet and continue to let steam until tender.

3. Place the beet and the apple, along with the cinnamon and clove, into a blender and process until smooth.

4. If needed, add water or juice from the steam for consistency.

5. Serve immediately or store in the refrigerator or freezer for a later date.

Vanilla Fig and Apple Puree

We love figs around our house, and this puree is a great combination your baby is going to love!

Ingredients

5 dried figs, stems removed (can use fresh when they are in season)

1 cup apple, diced (about 1 medium-size apple)

1 tsp. vanilla extract

2 cups water

Directions

1. Add all ingredients to a medium-size saucepan and bring to a boil.

2. Reduce heat and simmer for about 15 minutes until figs have been rehydrated and apples are tender.

3. Drain, then add ingredients to a blender and blend until smooth. Add more water for consistency if needed.

4. Serve immediately or store in the refrigerator or freezer for a later date.

Roasted Butternut Squash with Nutmeg

Butternut squash gets a boost of healthy fats from the added coconut oil, along with getting extra sweet in the oven while it roasts, making it ideal for your baby's palate.

Ingredients

2 cups butternut squash, peeled and diced

1 tbsp. coconut oil

½ tsp. nutmeg

Directions

1. Preheat oven to 400 degrees.

2. Toss butternut squash with melted coconut oil and nutmeg, and place on a parchment paper-lined baking sheet.

3. Roast for 30 minutes or until tender.

4. Place all ingredients in a blender and process until smooth.

5. Add water if needed for consistency.

6. Serve immediately or store in the refrigerator or freezer for a later date.

Zucchini Mashed Potatoes with Thyme

Thyme is one of my favorite herbs to use in baby food because it adds a delicious and mild flavor to any puree. Its delicate lemony flavor is the perfect pairing for these mashed potatoes with zucchini!

Ingredients

1 russet potato, peeled and chopped

2 green zucchini, peel left on, chopped (about 1 cup)

1 tsp. fresh thyme

1 tbsp. grass-fed butter

Pinch of black pepper

⅛–¼ cup homemade or low-sodium chicken stock

Directions

1. Add potato to a medium saucepan and cover with cold water.

2. Bring to a boil for 15–20 minutes, until tender.

3. The last 5 minutes of cook time, add chopped zucchini and thyme and let cook until soft.

4. Drain the potatoes and zucchini and add to a food processor; add butter, black pepper, and about half the chicken stock. Process until smooth. Add more stock if needed for consistency.

5. Serve immediately or store for a later date.

Roasted Banana and Pears with Cinnamon

I will go ahead and warn you that this recipe is extra delicious. By roasting the fruit, it becomes even sweeter and your baby is going to gobble it up quickly, which is totally fine because everything is good for them!

Ingredients

1 tbsp. coconut oil

1 large banana

1 cup pear, peeled and diced

½ tsp. cinnamon

Note: This is a recipe that I have continued to make and use in pancakes, oatmeal, and even spread on toast! It's really that delicious!

Directions

1. Preheat oven to 350 degrees.

2. Melt coconut oil and drizzle over the banana and pear.

3. Sprinkle with cinnamon, and place fruits on a parchment-lined baking sheet.

4. Roast for 15–20 minutes, until pear and banana are tender.

5. Add all ingredients to a blender and blend until smooth. Add water for consistency if needed.

6. Serve immediately or store for a later date.

Vanilla Ginger Asian Pears

I love using fresh ginger wherever I can because it's great for babies' tummies and for their developing immune systems. The combination of vanilla and ginger with the Asian pears is truly delicious.

Ingredients

2 cups Asian pears, peeled and diced (can substitute regular pears here too)

1 cup water

1 tsp. fresh ginger, grated

¼ tsp. pure vanilla extract

Directions

1. Place pears into a medium saucepan with the water, along with ginger and vanilla, and bring to a boil.

2. Cook until pears are tender, about 15 minutes.

3. Add pears to the blender along with a little bit of the water and blend until smooth.

4. Add a bit of the cooking liquid if necessary for consistency.

5. Serve immediately or store in the refrigerator or freezer for a later date.

Baby Kale, Peas, and Pears

The addition of pears in this recipe cuts through the harshness of the kale, giving it a sweetness that your baby will love. This puree is full of vitamins and nutrients for your little one!

Ingredients

1 cup water

1 cup baby kale (can substitute baby spinach)

½ cup peas

1 cup pear, diced and peeled (about 1 large pear)

Note: If the pear isn't ripe, simply cook it until it softens before adding to the blender.

Directions

1. Bring water to a boil in a medium saucepan, then add kale and peas for 2 minutes to quickly blanch the vegetables.

2. Strain the veggies, reserving ½ cup of liquid, and add kale and peas to the blender.

3. Add pear to the kale and peas along with half of the reserved liquid.

4. Blend until smooth, adding more liquid if necessary for consistency.

5. Serve immediately or store in the refrigerator or freezer for a later date.

Green Bean, Pear, and Tofu

Tofu is great for adding protein to your little one's diet. It's soft by nature, so it purees beautifully and is mild in flavor so it can pair with just about any other ingredient!

Ingredients

½ cup green beans

1 cup water

¼ cup soft tofu

½ cup very ripe pear

Directions

1. Boil green beans in water in a medium saucepan until they are tender, about 10 minutes.

2. Strain and add to a high-powered blender with the tofu and pear.

3. Blend until smooth. Add water for consistency if needed.

4. Serve immediately or store in the refrigerator or freezer for a later date.

Turnip Leek Mash

Turnips are higher in nutritional value than white potatoes, and can make a yummy alternative to mashed potatoes!

Ingredients

1 tbsp. grass-fed butter

1 leek, washed thoroughly and sliced

⅛ tsp. black pepper

2 cups turnips (about 2–3 large turnips)

Directions

1. In a small saucepan, add the butter along with leek and black pepper.

2. Cook for 5 minutes until leek is tender.

3. Meanwhile, peel the turnips and steam for 15–20 minutes until tender.

4. Add all ingredients to a food processor and blend until smooth.

5. Add stock if needed for consistency.

6. Serve immediately or store for a later date.

Roasted Carrots with Ginger and Pumpkin

Your baby is going to flip over this flavor-packed puree full of vitamins and healthy fats. Pumpkin and carrots are both great for developing eyesight, with their high content of beta-carotene, and taste even better with the addition of ginger, which is great for their tummies and immune systems!

Ingredients

4 carrots, peeled

1 tsp. coconut oil

½ cup pumpkin puree

1 tsp. fresh ginger, grated

Pinch of cinnamon

Directions

1. Preheat oven to 400 degrees.

2. Toss the whole carrots with coconut oil and roast for 30 minutes, or until tender.

3. In a high-powered blender or food processor, add roasted carrots, pumpkin puree, ginger, and cinnamon, and blend until smooth.

4. Serve immediately or store in the refrigerator or freezer for a later date.

Broccoli and Apple

Broccoli is one of those vegetables that can be a little harsh on its own for a baby's palate, but by adding a little sweetness from the apple, this combination is a winner!

Ingredients

1 cup fresh broccoli florets

1 cup apple, diced and peeled

Note: Broccoli can cause gas sometimes in little ones. I like to introduce broccoli early on in the day to ensure your baby doesn't end up with gas when they are trying to go to bed.

Directions

1. Steam broccoli and apple until tender, about 15 minutes.

2. Place into a high-powered blender and blend until smooth. Add water for consistency if needed.

3. Serve immediately or store in the refrigerator or freezer for a later date.

Cinnamon Stone Fruit Puree

Ingredients

2 ripe black plums

2 ripe apricots (can sub peaches)

¼ tsp. cinnamon

Note: If fruit isn't soft and ripe, cook the fruit in water over the stove to soften before adding to the blender.

Directions

1. Peel and pit plums. Remove the pits from the apricots.
2. Add both the plums and the apricots to the blender along with the cinnamon.
3. Blend until smooth.
4. Serve immediately or store in the refrigerator or freezer for a later date.

Creamy Mango and Yogurt

Mango is full of vitamin C, potassium, and several other vitamins so good for your baby! I love mixing it with yogurt to give it some protein and creaminess for a truly yummy and nutritious puree.

Ingredients

1 ripe mango, diced and peeled

1 tbsp. water (if needed for consistency)

½ cup Greek or plain yogurt

Directions

1. Blend mango in a food processor or blender until smooth. Add water if needed at this time.
2. Stir in yogurt and serve.
3. Serve immediately or store in the refrigerator or freezer for a later date.

Coconut Brown Rice and Lentil Puree

Lentils are packed with fiber, protein, and other necessary vitamins for your quickly-growing baby. Combining them with a tasty coconut brown rice makes for a delicious and hearty puree that is extremely healthy for your child!

Ingredients

1 cup brown rice

2 cups full-fat
    coconut milk

½ cup cooked lentils

Directions

1. Bring rice and coconut milk to a boil in a large saucepan.

2. Reduce the heat and cover, and let simmer for 45 minutes, until the rice is tender.

3. Add the coconut rice and the cooked lentils to a blender, adding water as needed for consistency, until smooth. (Puree should be left with a little texture.)

4. Serve immediately or store in the refrigerator or freezer for a later date.

Roasted Blueberries and Greek Yogurt

Roasting blueberries in this recipe makes them even sweeter and more delicious while the coconut oil gives your baby a good dose of healthy fats! These berries are perfect when combined with a creamy yogurt to make the prettiest of purees.

Ingredients

2 cups blueberries

1 tbsp. coconut oil

½ cup Greek yogurt

Directions

1. Preheat oven to 350 degrees.

2. Toss blueberries in melted coconut oil and spread evenly onto a parchment-lined baking sheet.

3. Roast the berries for 15 minutes until the berries burst. Let cool.

4. Add Greek yogurt and roasted blueberries to a blender and process until smooth.

5. Serve immediately or store in the refrigerator or freezer for a later date.

Black Bean and Dark Cherry Puree

Cherries and black beans actually mix harmoniously together in this creamy puree your baby will love, giving them a good dose of protein and vitamins essential for their little bodies!

Ingredients

½ cup black beans, rinsed and drained

1 cup pitted dark cherries

Directions

1. Place all ingredients into a blender and process until smooth.

2. Add water if needed for consistency.

3. Serve immediately or store in the refrigerator or freezer for a later date.

Cinnamon Applesauce

I would recommend making a large batch of this recipe to keep in your refrigerator because you will go through it quickly! It will definitely be one of your child's favorites from the infant stage through their toddler years.

Ingredients

2 cups apples, chopped and peeled (peeling optional if using organic)

1 tsp. cinnamon

2 cups water

Directions

1. Place apples and cinnamon in water in a medium saucepan, and bring to a boil.

2. Boil until apples are tender, about 15 minutes.

3. Blend until smooth.

4. Serve immediately or store in the refrigerator or freezer for a later date.

Smoothie Sips

8+ months

Smoothies aren't just for adults anymore! They are also gaining popularity among parents everywhere for their children because they taste great and have such a high nutritional value when you make them right. I started giving Parks smoothies early on since I could make them with so many good ingredients that his body needed, all packed into one glass. I feel great knowing he gets a good amount of the recommended daily servings of fruits and vegetables by simply drinking one smoothie! No matter what the age of your child, smoothies are the perfect way to get all the good stuff in them in one sitting. You can bet there won't be any objections to eating their veggies in this chapter!

You can get as creative as you want with smoothies, and the consistency is just right for babies and toddlers alike. You can add in as many nutrient-packed ingredients as you desire and will always know that you are doing something really fantastic for your kids.

My rule for smoothies, to keep them healthy, is to never add any refined sugar, only fruit and sometimes honey (if your child is over one year of age) for any added sweetness. When you add in vegetables, it makes them even healthier and your kids will not even realize that they could be drinking a whole two cups of spinach or kale in just one drink.

Smoothie time has become a part of our regular midmorning routine after we return home from the gym for a perfect healthy and energizing snack. As soon as my son hears the blender going, he comes running and gets so excited about what he is about to have! I just love his enthusiasm for them, and that he is gulping down things like spinach and turmeric that are giving his body so many vitamins.

The idea of starting out the day with smoothies as part of a healthy breakfast is great, but even if your smoothie time isn't a daily occurrence, it's a great thing to add into your weekend routine as a family. Get your toddler involved in smoothie time by letting them add ingredients to the blender or get items out of the fridge, to make it a family affair. It's so fun and important to get your kids excited and eager to help with the preparation of food from an early age so they feel invested in their health and the food they are eating!

Smoothies are the perfect way to get everyone, young and old, involved and excited about healthy food that tastes really amazing! We love sharing smoothies in our house as a family and I think you will love making this a part of your household too.

I have put together some of my favorite, go-to smoothie recipes that have us looking forward to smoothie time every day of the week!

Recipes

Note: Smoothie recipes make 1–2 servings, making it ideal to split with your baby or toddler.

Cinnamon Banana and Peanut Butter Oat Smoothie

This smoothie is a delicious combination and is perfect for breakfast in place of your kiddo's regular bowl of oatmeal. Peanut butter and banana are meant for each other and they get an extra delicious flavor burst with the addition of cinnamon!

Ingredients

1 frozen banana

1 tbsp. peanut butter (or nut butter of your choice)

¼ cup rolled oats

¼ cup plain kefir

½ cup unsweetened vanilla almond milk (or milk of your choice)

1 tsp. cinnamon

4 ice cubes

Directions

1. Place all ingredients into a blender and process until smooth.

2. Serve immediately.

Note: Kefir is a drink made from milk that is fermented with healthy bacteria that is great for your baby's tummy and immune health. The taste is similar to a plain yogurt.

Coconut Apricot Persimmon Smoothie with Ginger

Persimmons are an abundant source of vitamins B6, C, and A, and are such a great addition to your baby's diet. Not only is the color of this smoothie amazing, but it's also an immune-boosting powerhouse with the addition of fresh ginger!

Ingredients

1 persimmon, peeled

2 ripe apricots, pitted and peeled

1 tsp. fresh ginger, grated

1 tbsp. shredded unsweetened coconut

½ cup unsweetened vanilla almond milk

4 ice cubes

Directions

1. Place all ingredients into a blender and blend until smooth.

2. Serve immediately.

Blackberry and Coconut Yogurt Smoothie

This gorgeous, light-purple smoothie is a great mix of creamy, sweet, and tart, giving your child plenty of delicious tastes! Blackberries are high in vitamins C and K and have a high fiber content too, making this extra healthy for anyone in the family!

Ingredients

¼ cup blackberries (frozen or fresh)

1 tbsp. unsweetened coconut, shredded

½ cup plain yogurt or kefir

½ cup unsweetened vanilla almond milk

1 tsp. honey (optional for babies over 1 year)

1 tbsp. chia seeds

¼ tsp. maca powder

1 tbsp. hemp protein or seeds

4 ice cubes

Directions

1. Place all ingredients into a blender and process until smooth.

2. Serve immediately.

Note: Maca powder is a supplement that is known to boost your child's calcium intake as well as improve learning and memory. It can also balance hormones, which has a positive effect on a child's behavior.

Healthy Peanut Butter and Jelly Smoothie

This one is such a fun take on a classic childhood flavor, turned into a healthy smoothie that your baby will drink up in a heartbeat. You can feel good about them drinking this at any time of the day.

Ingredients

1 frozen banana

1 tbsp. peanut butter

1 tbsp. Strawberry Chia Jam (page 133) (or jam of your choice)

¼ cup plain kefir

½ cup unsweetened vanilla almond milk (or milk of your choice)

1 tsp. honey (optional for babies over 1 year)

4 ice cubes

Directions

1. Place all ingredients into a blender and process until smooth.

2. Serve immediately.

Creamsicle Smoothie

A creamsicle is a favorite flavor from my childhood that is made healthy and delicious in my new take on it in smoothie form. You can feel great knowing that your baby is getting a good dose of probiotics as well as vitamin C from this yummy drink! This one is going to be a favorite in your house among the whole family, perfect for a fresh start to any day!

Ingredients

1 orange

1 frozen banana

½ cup kefir

½ cup unsweetened vanilla almond milk

1 tsp. honey (for babies over 1 year, otherwise use maple syrup)

4 ice cubes

Directions

1. Place all ingredients into a blender and process until smooth.

2. Serve immediately.

Coconut Mango Smoothie

Mango is a great source of vitamins A and C and is loaded with fiber too! It pairs perfectly with creamy yogurt and banana to make a delicious, tropical smoothie that every child is sure to love.

Ingredients

⅓ cup mango, peeled and diced

⅛ cup unsweetened coconut

½ cup almond milk

2 tbsp. plain Greek yogurt

1 tbsp. honey (for babies over 1 year)

½ frozen banana

4 ice cubes

Directions

1. Place all ingredients into a blender and process until smooth.

2. Serve immediately.

Green Machine Avocado Smoothie

Avocados are so healthy for kids of all ages, as they ensure a good amount of healthy fats perfect for growing bodies. I love the addition of spinach to make this an extra-green and vitamin-packed smoothie that is honestly delicious!

Ingredients

¼ avocado

½ cup baby spinach

½ frozen banana

½ cup almond milk

1 tbsp. hemp seeds

1 tsp. honey (for babies over 1 year)

4 ice cubes

Directions

1. Place all ingredients into a blender and process until smooth.

2. Serve immediately.

Beet and Strawberry Smoothie

Beets are a superfood for babies due to their high vitamin and phytonutrient content. I love adding them into recipes like smoothies because of their nutritional boost and gorgeous color! I promise that your kiddo will slurp them down no problem in this delicious smoothie!

Ingredients

1 beet, peeled and diced
(about ¼ cup)

4 strawberries

8 oz. coconut water

2 tbsp. Greek yogurt

½ cup baby spinach

1 tbsp. walnuts

1 tbsp. chia seeds

4 ice cubes

Directions:

1. Place all ingredients into a blender and process until smooth.

2. Serve immediately.

Cocoa Spinach Protein Smoothie

You won't believe how much this smoothie tastes like a chocolate milk shake! This smoothie, unlike a milk shake, is made with zero refined sugars and is given a nutritional boost with a full cup of spinach. This recipe is going to be a favorite with your toddler—and the rest of the family too!

Ingredients

1 cup baby spinach

1 tbsp. unsweetened cocoa powder

1 tbsp. whey protein or plant protein

1 frozen banana

½ cup unsweetened vanilla almond milk

¼ cup plain kefir or Greek yogurt

1 tsp. honey (optional for babies over 1 year)

1 tsp. chia seeds

1 tbsp. hemp seeds

4–6 ice cubes

Directions

1. Place all ingredients into a blender and process until smooth.

2. Serve immediately.

Roasted Cinnamon Sweet Potato Smoothie

When you roast a sweet potato, it becomes sweet and decadent, making it the perfect addition to a delicious smoothie! This smoothie tastes like a sweet potato pie without any of the bad ingredients like refined sugar. It's made with ingredients that are so good for your baby, and I can guarantee that you will be roasting up extra sweet potatoes to have on hand just for making smoothies!

Ingredients

½ cup sweet potato, peeled and roasted

½ cup unsweetened vanilla almond milk

1 tsp. ground cinnamon

½ frozen banana

¼ cup kefir

1 tsp. maple syrup

4 ice cubes

Directions

1. Place all ingredients into a blender and process until smooth.

2. Serve immediately.

Pineapple Kale Smoothie

Pineapple is considered one of the world's healthiest foods because it's known for having a high content of fiber and vitamins, among other things. It sweetens up the kale just perfectly to make one extra-healthy smoothie that your baby or toddler is going to love.

Ingredients

¼ cup fresh or frozen pineapple

½ cup fresh kale

½ cup coconut water

1 tsp. chia seeds

1 tsp. bee pollen

1½ frozen bananas

4 ice cubes

Directions

1. Place all ingredients into a blender and process until smooth.

2. Serve immediately.

Cherry and Kale Kefir Smoothie

Cherries and kale are such great sources of essential vitamins for your child, and combined they make this a superfood power smoothie that will fill your baby with his or her daily dose of vitamin C, calcium, fiber, and so much more! Drink up!

Ingredients

½ cup fresh or frozen dark cherries, pitted

½ cup kale, chopped

1 cup kefir

½ frozen banana

½ cup coconut water

1 tbsp. hemp seeds (optional)

4 ice cubes

Directions

1. Place all ingredients into a blender and process until smooth.

2. Serve immediately.

Kale and Berry Peanut Butter Smoothie

Kale might not sound like it would be peanut butter's best friend, but these two ingredients combined with frozen berries make one delicious drink that your baby (and you) are going to love! This flavor combination is a favorite in our house.

Ingredients

1 cup baby kale

½ frozen banana

1 tsp. peanut butter (or nut butter of your choice)

4 oz. coconut water

1 tsp. chia seeds

1 tsp. hemp seeds

¼ cup frozen mixed berries (can use fresh berries too)

4 ice cubes

Directions

1. Place all ingredients into a blender and blend until smooth.

2. Serve immediately.

Pomegranate, Raspberry, and Chia Smoothie

Did you know that pomegranates are loaded with antioxidants and vitamins? That means this smoothie is not only gorgeous and tasty, but it's also packed with seriously good stuff that your baby or toddler needs! Doesn't get much better that this smoothie right here.

Ingredients

1 tbsp. pomegranate seeds or juice

5 raspberries

¼ cup plain whole-milk yogurt

½ cup unsweetened vanilla almond milk

½ frozen banana

1 tbsp. chia seeds

1 tsp. honey (for babies over 1 year)

4 ice cubes

Directions

1. Place all ingredients into a blender and process until smooth.

2. Serve immediately.

Turmeric "Golden Milk" Smoothie

Golden milk is gaining popularity thanks to its use of turmeric, which has anti-inflammatory properties, boosts the immune system, and is thought of as a cancer-preventing spice too. That's why I love turning this drink into a smoothie perfect for little ones! It has a tangy kick from the fresh turmeric that gets mellowed out from coconut milk and a creamy banana, making it pleasing to your little one's taste buds. This is another smoothie that the whole family will love and should be drinking on a regular basis!

Ingredients

1-inch piece fresh turmeric, peeled (or 1 tsp. ground turmeric)

½ cup coconut milk (or milk of your choice)

1 frozen banana

1 tsp. cinnamon

¼ tsp. fresh or ground ginger

1 tsp. honey (for babies over 1 year) or maple syrup

4 ice cubes

Directions

1. Place all ingredients into a blender and process until smooth.
2. Serve immediately.

Note: To make any smoothie dairy-free, simply swap yogurt or milk for a dairy-free version or omit altogether. To make any smoothie nut-free, simply omit the nut butter or nuts used in the smoothie! These recipes can be altered to fit the dietary needs of your family.

Breakfast Bowls

9+ months

Breakfast is the most important meal of the day, if you ask me, and it really sets the tone for how the rest of the day is going to go. Starting my son's day out with a breakfast that is really good for him and that doesn't take me long to prepare sets us up for a good morning all around!

That's why I love breakfast bowls of all varieties—they are usually quick and easy recipes that are made mostly with ingredients that you always have in your fridge and pantry! This prepares you for a successful start to any day.

I love that whether you consider yourself a cook or not, or even enjoy cooking, for that matter, anyone can make a breakfast bowl. This quality alone makes them ideal for any parent trying to ensure their child has a healthy start to their day.

From overnight oats, breakfast hash, yogurt bowls, and tofu scrambles, there are plenty of options to keep your baby from getting bored with the same old breakfast every morning of the week. Kids like variety and having a few go-to recipes that you like to rotate sure makes getting them to eat what you put in front of them that much easier!

Tips: To make any recipe non-dairy, simply substitute milk for a non-dairy version and yogurt can be subbed for a non-dairy version such as soy or coconut yogurt.

To make any of these recipes gluten-free, simply swap the grain being used for a gluten-free version if desired. There are several gluten-free oat options out there in your regular supermarket.

Recipes

Overnight Pumpkin Pie Oats

Serves 1

It doesn't get much easier than overnight oats! These are a mama's dream because you can literally have them in front of your kiddo ready to eat in under sixty seconds since you did all the heavy lifting the night before. I have a few of these in my fridge every week for mornings when you need breakfast on the table quick!

Ingredients
½ cup rolled oats

1 tbsp. Greek yogurt

¾ cup whole milk (can sub
  another non-dairy milk)

2 tbsp. pumpkin puree

1 tsp. pumpkin pie spice

½ tsp. ground cinnamon

Pinch of salt

1 tbsp. maple syrup or
  honey (for babies over
  1 year)

Directions
1. Combine all ingredients in a mason jar and stir to combine.

2. Refrigerate overnight and serve as is the next morning or heat before serving.

3. Jars can be kept in the refrigerator for up to one week.

Strawberry Cocoa Chia Pudding

Serves 1

Chia pudding is the perfect toddler and baby breakfast (or snack). Its thick and creamy consistency goes great with any fresh fruit or flavor combination and is packed with omega-3s and healthy fats for your growing babe! I love the combination of strawberry and cocoa and it's sure to have your kiddo asking for seconds.

Ingredients

½ cup full-fat coconut milk (or milk of your choice)

⅛ cup chia seeds

2 tbsp. cocoa powder

1 tbsp. maple syrup

2 diced strawberries

Directions

1. Combine coconut milk, chia seeds, cocoa powder, and maple syrup in a mason jar and stir to combine.

2. Refrigerate for at least two hours or up to overnight.

3. Top with fresh strawberries and serve.

4. Chia pudding will keep in the refrigerator for up to a week prior to toppings being added.

Blackberry Farro Yogurt Parfait

Serves 1

Farro is a great whole grain to incorporate into your child's diet. I love adding it to yogurt bowls to make them a little heartier and more filling! This combination is a winner that your baby or toddler is sure to love.

Ingredients

¼ cup cooked farro (can substitute quinoa)

½ cup plain whole-milk Greek yogurt

¼ cup fresh blackberries

1 tsp. honey (optional for babies over 1 year) or maple syrup

Directions

1. Layer farro, yogurt, blackberries, and honey in a glass or bowl. Serve immediately.

2. These parfaits can be prepped the night before and kept in the refrigerator for 2–3 days.

Peaches and Cream Steel Cut Oats

Serves 1

Peaches are always a favorite fruit with children. I love adding them into oatmeal with a little kefir to make a delicious bowl of oatmeal containing healthy probiotics that my son loves!

Ingredients

¾ cup water

¼ cup steel cut oats

¼ cup unsweetened vanilla almond milk

½ tsp. pure vanilla extract

1 tsp. maple syrup

¼ cup peaches, diced and peeled

2 tbsp. plain kefir or yogurt

Directions

1. Bring water to a boil, then stir in oats and let cook for 2–3 minutes.

2. Add almond milk, vanilla extract, maple syrup, and peaches and continue to cook until oats have thickened and are tender, about five more minutes.

3. To serve, drizzle kefir over the oats and serve immediately.

Carrot Cake Oatmeal

This oatmeal tastes just like a slice of carrot cake without all that sugar! The bonus here is that your baby will be getting extra vitamins from the carrots, plus they will absolutely love the taste of it. If I had to guess, you will probably find yourself making a bowl of this for yourself, too!

Ingredients

1 tsp. coconut oil

¼ cup grated and peeled carrot

½ cup old-fashioned oats

¾ cup unsweetened vanilla almond milk, plus more for serving

1 tsp. cinnamon

⅛ tsp. nutmeg

1 tsp. maple syrup or brown sugar

Pinch of salt

Directions

1. Heat a small saucepan over medium heat and add the coconut oil.

2. Add the carrot to the oil and cook for 2–3 minutes until it begins to soften.

3. Add the oats and milk to the pot and bring to a boil.

4. Stir in cinnamon, nutmeg, syrup, and salt, then reduce the heat and let simmer 10–15 minutes until the oatmeal has thickened.

5. Serve the oatmeal immediately and drizzle with extra almond milk before serving.

Vanilla Citrus Yogurt Bowls

Serves 1

I am a huge fan of not buying store-bought flavored yogurts for my son. Most of them are loaded with sugar and you can make an even more delicious homemade version. I love the combination of citrus and vanilla—these yogurt bowls are going to be your kid's favorite!

Ingredients

½ cup plain whole-milk Greek yogurt

½ tsp. orange zest

1 tbsp. fresh orange juice

¼ tsp. vanilla extract (optional, can sub vanilla beans here)

¼ cup fresh orange slices or segments

1 tbsp. chia seeds

Granola (optional for babies/toddlers with more teeth)

Directions

1. Combine yogurt, orange zest, orange juice, and vanilla extract in a small bowl and whisk well.

2. Top the flavored yogurt with fresh orange slices, chia seeds, and granola, if using.

3. Serve immediately or prep the flavored yogurt in advance and simply add toppings when ready to serve.

Olive Oil and Parmesan Savory Oats

Serves 1

Oatmeal doesn't always have to be served in a sweet version. In fact, I happen to love a good bowl of savory oats! These cheesy oats drizzled with olive oil give your little one a good source of healthy fats and is a delicious new take on his or her regular bowl of morning oatmeal.

Ingredients

¼ cup rolled oats

½ cup milk or water

1 tbsp. grated Parmesan cheese (can substitute white cheddar cheese)

1 tsp. chia seeds

1 tsp. olive oil

Pinch of kosher salt

Pinch of black pepper

Directions

1. Place oats and liquid in a microwave-safe bowl and cook until thickened. Or, cook them on the stove by bringing to a boil and reducing heat until oats have thickened.

2. Sprinkle with Parmesan cheese, chia seeds, drizzle with olive oil, and sprinkle with salt and pepper and stir to combine.

3. Serve immediately.

Strawberry Jam and Pineapple Cottage Cheese Bowls

Serves 1

Cottage cheese is full of protein and can be eaten as a perfect snack or breakfast that your little one will love! With the addition of fruit and chia seeds, these bowls are perfect for a nutritious start to the day.

Ingredients

2 tbsp. Strawberry Chia Jam (page 133) (or jam of your choice)

½ cup cottage cheese

¼ cup fresh pineapple, diced

1 tbsp. chia seeds

Directions

1. Layer jam, cottage cheese, and pineapple in a bowl and sprinkle with chia seeds.

2. Serve immediately or store in mason jars for easy make-ahead breakfasts.

Boiled Egg Mash

Serves 1–2

Growing up, my mom always made me boiled eggs that she would mash with butter, salt, and pepper in a bowl, and I still eat it to this day! It is truly so simple, yet so delicious. I started making my son the same thing pretty early on because it was soft enough for him to eat with little teeth, and it made sure he was getting a good amount of protein at the beginning of the day.

Ingredients
2 eggs

1 tbsp. grass-fed butter

¼ tsp. black pepper

Pinch of kosher or sea salt

Note: If you or your family have a history of an egg allergy, start with only the yolk of the egg when introducing to baby as the egg white has proteins that are more likely to cause an allergic reaction.

Directions
1. Boil eggs until the yolk is cooked through, about 12 minutes.
2. Peel eggs and mash with a fork while hot.
3. Add butter, pepper, and salt to the egg mash and continue mixing until butter has melted.
4. Serve immediately.

Overnight Apple Cinnamon Oats

Serves 1

This apple cinnamon version is another great option for overnight oats that can make your life a whole lot easier on busy mornings. I like to make Cinnamon Applesauce (page 51) in bulk to keep in the fridge at all times to add into recipes like these oats!

Ingredients

½ cup rolled oats

¾ cup unsweetened almond milk

¼ cup unsweetened applesauce or Cinnamon Applesauce (page 51)

1 tsp. cinnamon

1 tsp. maple syrup (optional)

Directions

1. Combine all ingredients into a mason jar the night before you want to eat it. Stir to combine thoroughly.

2. Serve the next morning with fresh apples or as is. You can serve the oats cold or they can be heated through.

3. Oats will store in the refrigerator for up to a week.

Quinoa and Oat Muesli

Serves 1

Mixing grains is a great way to introduce new textures and incorporate different whole grains into your baby's diet. This muesli is full of nutrients and is perfect for your baby or toddler any day of the week!

Ingredients

¼ cup quinoa

¼ cup rolled oats

¾ cup almond milk

½ cup water

1 tsp. pure vanilla extract

1 tsp. maple syrup

1 tbsp. raisins

Fresh fruit (I used finely diced apples)

Dash of cinnamon

Directions

1. Add quinoa, oats, almond milk, water, and vanilla into a small saucepan and bring to a boil.

2. Reduce heat and simmer for fifteen minutes until muesli has thickened and cooked through.

3. Drizzle with maple syrup and top with raisins, fresh fruit, and a dash of cinnamon and serve immediately.

Zucchini Steel Cut Oatmeal Bowls

Serves 1–2

Zucchini is pretty mild in flavor, so it's the perfect addition for many baked goods and even oatmeal!

Ingredients
¾ cup water

¼ cup steel cut oats

¼ cup zucchini, grated

1 tsp. cinnamon

1 tsp. coconut oil

1 tsp. honey (for babies over 1 year) or maple syrup

Directions
1. Bring water to a boil and stir in oats.
2. Reduce heat and then stir in zucchini and let the oatmeal thicken, about 5 minutes.
3. Sprinkle in cinnamon, and then stir in coconut oil and honey.
4. Serve immediately.

Apple, Sweet Potato, and Turkey Sausage Hash Bowls

Serves 1–2

This hash is perfect for breakfast, lunch, or dinner! Your babe is going to love this slightly sweet and savory bowl of goodness. A hash is such a great way to start your child's day!

Ingredients

1 cup sweet potato, diced

1 tbsp. avocado or olive oil

¼ cup onion, finely diced

¼ cup apple, diced

2 organic turkey sausage links, diced

1 tsp. kosher salt

½ tsp. black pepper

1 tsp. maple syrup

Directions

1. Boil sweet potato for 5 minutes until just soft, but not cooked all the way through. Drain and set aside.

2. Heat oil in a skillet over medium heat and add onion and apple.

3. Cook for 2–3 minutes, then add in sweet potato and diced sausage.

4. Season with salt and pepper and cook for another 10 minutes, stirring occasionally, until potato is tender and sausage is cooked through. Place lid on in between stirring the hash to steam the potato and continue to cook through.

5. Drizzle with maple syrup and serve immediately.

Southwestern Tofu Scramble Bowls

Serves 3–6

Tofu is a great option if your baby has an egg allergy or if you want a vegetarian option to add into their diet. It can take on any flavor, and honestly tastes very similar to an egg when scrambled! The southwestern spices in this recipe add so much flavor to this dish and your baby or toddler is going to love this one.

Ingredients

1 tbsp. avocado or vegetable oil

¼ cup onion, finely diced

12 oz. extra-firm tofu, patted dry

1 tsp. cumin

1 tsp. chili powder

1 tsp. turmeric

¼ tsp. garlic powder

¼ tsp. paprika

1 tsp. kosher salt

½ tsp. black pepper

2–3 tbsp. water

½ cup black beans, drained and rinsed

1 avocado, diced

1 tbsp. cilantro, chopped (optional)

Directions

1. Heat oil in a large skillet.
2. Add onion to the oil and sauté for 2–3 minutes until it becomes translucent.
3. Crumble tofu and add to the onion, and cook for another couple of minutes.
4. Mix cumin, chili powder, turmeric, garlic powder, paprika, salt, and pepper in a small bowl. Add water and mix to create a sauce.
5. Pour spice mixture over the tofu and stir to coat everything evenly.
6. Add black beans to the tofu and stir. Cook for another five minutes.
7. To serve, top with fresh avocado pieces and cilantro.

Note: This recipe makes 3–6 servings. You can freeze leftovers in individual portions or serve as a family breakfast!

Creamy Cheddar Spinach Grits Bowls

Serves 3–6

Growing up in the South, grits were a part of our breakfasts quite a bit. Grits are a great food for little ones because they are a perfect texture for babies with teeth or without. I like adding in cheese and spinach to make the perfect well-balanced breakfast bowl!

Ingredients

2 cups water (or milk)

2 tsp. kosher or sea salt

½ cup old-fashioned grits
   (can sub polenta here)

2 tbsp. whole milk or cream
   (optional)

¼ cup cheddar cheese,
   shredded

2 tbsp. grass-fed butter or
   ghee

½ cup fresh spinach, finely
   chopped

½ tsp. black pepper

Directions

1. Bring water (or milk) to a boil.

2. Add 1 teaspoon of salt to the water and whisk in grits to prevent clumping.

3. Cook until grits have thickened.

4. Pour in milk or cream and combine.

5. Melt in cheese and butter, then wilt the spinach by stirring into the grits.

6. Season with the rest of the salt and pepper.

7. Serve with extra butter if desired.

Note: This recipe makes 3–6 portions. You can freeze into individual portions. To make this recipe dairy-free, omit the milk, cheese, and butter.

Mini Bites

10+ months

As your baby starts to get the hang of this "eating solid food" thing, the fun really begins! This is the stage when they are going to start wanting everything you are eating right off your plate, so you might as well be making them goodies you would want to eat too!

This chapter of little bites is perfect for the next stage of your baby's eating, where they will begin to eat foods with more textures and begin feeding themselves as well. Finger foods and foods that are easily chewed are best for this stage, as most babies don't have very many teeth yet.

I get so happy about babies that are excited about eating! Parks absolutely loves to eat and has since he first tasted real food! I attribute his love of food to the exposure I gave him to healthy and delicious food from the beginning. I don't shy away from letting him taste whatever it is I'm eating if he is interested, and I try to let him play in the kitchen while I am cooking as much as possible so he

can start to love it as much as I do. I truly believe that if kids grow up learning about food, where it comes from, and how it's prepared, that they will have a greater appreciation for what they are putting in their bodies throughout their lives!

I think one of the biggest mistakes we can make as parents is assuming our kids might not like a certain flavor or recipe. Don't assume your little one won't like something just because you don't, or because you think it is too advanced in flavor for them, because they just might surprise you! I don't shy away from using ingredients like onions, garlic, and a variety of spices (not the *heat* spicy kind) whenever I cook for my son. You as the cook in your own house can always alter a recipe to make it work for your kiddo's taste buds. If you have a little one that doesn't like garlic or curry or whatever is in any recipe, swap it for something they will like or omit it altogether! You get to be in charge in your kitchen and that is what is so great about making homemade food for your family.

I have combined all my favorite recipes for babies who are ready to graduate from purees and enter into a new world of exciting textures and flavors. I think you and your little one are really going to start having fun (and making messes) together!

Recipes

White Bean and Pea Hummus

Serves 6–8

Hummus is the perfect snack or addition to any baby's meal! My white bean and pea hummus is packed with nutrition and is a fun twist on a classic that your baby (and the rest of your family) will love. I love having this recipe in the fridge for healthy snacks all week long.

Ingredients

1 cup frozen peas, thawed

15-oz. can white beans, drained and rinsed

1 tbsp. tahini paste

2 tbsp. lemon juice

1 small garlic clove (optional)

1 tsp. kosher salt

½ tsp. black pepper

¼ cup olive oil

Whole wheat pita, for dipping (optional)

Directions

1. Place all ingredients into a food processor and process until smooth. Add a little water if needed for consistency.

2. Taste and adjust salt and pepper as needed.

3. Dip pita into hummus to serve or serve the hummus alone with a spoon.

Spiced Avocado Toast Sticks

Serves 2

Who doesn't love a good piece of avocado toast? It's such a great breakfast, lunch, or snack, and is ideal for babies and toddlers alike! Let your babe hop onboard the avocado toast train with my spiced avocado toast sticks, perfect for little ones learning to feed themselves!

Ingredients

½ ripe avocado

¼ tsp. chili powder

⅛ tsp. black pepper

½ tsp. lemon juice

Pinch of kosher or sea salt (optional)

2 slices whole wheat sprouted bread

Directions

1. Smash avocado, chili powder, black pepper, lemon juice, and salt together in a small bowl until well combined.

2. Toast the bread for a few minutes until warm, careful not to get too toasty.

3. Spread the avocado evenly on each piece of bread and cut into strips. Remove crust if baby has a hard time chewing it.

Mini Whole Wheat Pancakes 3 Ways

Serves 1–2 each

These pancakes will be a favorite of your baby! With three different flavor combinations, this is a breakfast packed full of good ingredients that your babe will never tire of!

Pumpkin Pancakes
1 egg
1 tbsp. Greek yogurt
2 tbsp. pumpkin puree
2 tbsp. whole wheat flour
⅛ tsp. baking powder
¼ tsp. cinnamon

Apple Banana Pancakes
1 egg
1 tbsp. Greek yogurt
1 tbsp. unsweetened
  applesauce
¼ mashed banana
¼ tsp. cinnamon
⅛ tsp. baking powder
2 tbsp. whole wheat flour

Blueberry Pancakes
1 egg
12 blueberries
2 tbsp. Greek yogurt
¼ tsp. vanilla extract
2 tbsp. whole wheat flour
⅛ tsp. baking powder

Directions
1. Combine all wet ingredients in a bowl and combine well. Add in dry ingredients and mix until just combined.
2. Heat a nonstick skillet over medium heat and add a little butter or coconut oil to the pan.
3. Place batter onto the skillet in 4 equal portions. Cook on one side until the top of the pancake has bubbles in it, about 3–5 minutes.
4. Flip the pancakes and cook for another 2 minutes on the other side.
5. Serve with Greek yogurt, bananas, or maple syrup.

Hint: Make extra of these and freeze for super easy and busy mornings!

Spinach and Lentil Fritters

Makes 6 fritters

Delicious and full of two baby superfoods, lentils and spinach, these fritters are not only good for your little one, but they will love the taste too!

Ingredients

1 cup lentils, cooked

½ cup baby spinach

2 tbsp. bread crumbs

1 egg

1 tsp. salt

½ tsp. black pepper

1 tbsp. olive oil

Note: Fritters store well in the freezer for easy snacks or meals.

Directions

1. Combine lentils and spinach in a food processor and pulse until combined.

2. Add bread crumbs, egg, salt, and pepper into the mix at this time, and pulse until all ingredients have come together.

3. Form the mixture into small patties.

4. Heat olive oil over medium heat in a nonstick pan and cook on each side for about 5 minutes, until golden brown.

Cheesy Corn and Scallion Cakes

Makes 12–15 cakes

Corn and scallions go perfectly together in this take on a savory pancake. Serve them as a side or on their own with a little grass-fed butter and your baby will gobble them up!

Ingredients

2 cups corn bread mix (or ¾ cup corn meal, 1¼ cups all-purpose flour + 1 tsp. baking powder)

1¼ cups milk

1 egg

½ cup cheddar cheese, shredded

3 tablespoons scallions, thinly sliced

1 cup fresh corn kernels

3 tablespoons avocado oil (or nonstick spray)

Directions

1. Mix all ingredients (except oil) together in a bowl.

2. Preheat a nonstick skillet over medium heat. Add avocado oil or brush with butter.

3. Place 2 tablespoons of the mixture at a time on the skillet and cook for 2–3 minutes per side until golden brown and cooked through.

4. Serve immediately or store in the freezer for easy snacks or an easy side for any meal.

Nut Butter and Strawberry Chia Jam Mini Sandwich Bites

Makes 1 sandwich

With no refined sugar, these mini sandwiches are good for your babe and I promise they will become a staple in your house! Make a batch of the jam to keep on hand in the refrigerator for easy breakfasts and lunches any day of the week.

Ingredients

2 cups fresh strawberries, hulled

¼ cup water

2 tbsp. chia seeds

1 tbsp. agave or maple syrup (optional—you might not need this if berries are super sweet)

Whole wheat bread (can sub gluten free bread)

2 tbsp. almond butter or nut butter of choice

Note: I love making this jam not only for peanut butter and jelly sandwiches but to top yogurts, oatmeal, and so much more! The jam will keep in the refrigerator for up to two weeks, but I guarantee it won't last that long!

Directions

1. Slice strawberries and add to a saucepan with the water.

2. Heat on medium until strawberries start to break down, and then add chia seeds to the pan.

3. Let the jam thicken from the chia seeds, about 10 minutes, and remove from the heat.

4. Chill thoroughly, a minimum of two hours but up to overnight.

5. Layer a bit of jam on one side of the bread and layer the almond butter on the other side and sandwich bread together.

6. Cut out mini sandwiches by slicing into 1-inch cubes and serve.

Roasted Curry Coconut Carrot Fries with a Yogurt Mint Dipping Sauce

Serves 3–4

Expand your baby's palate with exotic flavors using my roasted curry coconut carrot fries and a delicious mint sauce. Your baby will love this new and healthy take on fries that are packed full of vitamins!

Ingredients

6 carrots, peeled

1 tbsp. coconut oil

1 tsp. curry powder

¼ tsp. black pepper

¼ tsp. salt

¼ cup Greek yogurt

1 tsp. fresh mint, chopped

1 tsp. lemon juice

Directions

1. Preheat oven to 400 degrees.
2. Slice carrots in half and then into ¼-inch strips to create fries.
3. Melt the coconut oil and drizzle over the carrots.
4. Sprinkle with curry powder, black pepper, and salt, and toss to combine with oil and seasonings.
5. Roast for 20–30 minutes, until carrots are tender and caramelized.
6. Meanwhile, combine yogurt, mint, and lemon juice in a small bowl and set aside.
7. Serve carrots alongside the yogurt sauce.

Lemon Basil Chickpeas

Serves 3–4

Chickpeas are loaded with protein and are the perfect finger food to help promote a baby's pincer grasp! I love serving them for a healthy snack or alongside any meal as a healthy side dish.

Ingredients

1 (15-oz.) can chickpeas,
   drained and rinsed

1 tbsp. avocado or olive oil

1 tbsp. fresh basil, chopped

1 tsp. lemon juice

⅛ tsp. kosher or sea salt

½ tsp. black pepper

Directions

1. Remove the skins from the chickpeas as they can be hard for babies to chew. The skins should rub off easily.

2. In a medium bowl, combine oil, basil, lemon, salt, and pepper, and whisk to combine.

3. Toss chickpeas in vinaigrette and serve immediately or store in the fridge for 2–3 days.

Mini Zucchini Muffins

Makes 24 mini muffins

We have a batch of these muffins in our freezer at all times—they are perfect for easy snacks, or on-the-go breakfasts when you find yourself in a pinch. They are packed with good-for-your babe ingredients and you can bet they will be a family favorite in your house for everyone!

Ingredients

1 cup all-purpose flour

1 cup whole wheat flour

½ tsp. baking powder

½ tsp. baking soda

½ tsp. ground cinnamon

1 cup zucchini, grated

1 banana, mashed

⅓ cup olive oil or melted coconut oil

¼ cup maple syrup (optional)

1 tsp. vanilla extract

1 egg

Directions

1. Preheat oven to 350 degrees. Prepare your mini muffin tray with paper liners (or spray with nonstick cooking spray).

2. Combine both flours, baking powder, baking soda, and cinnamon in a large bowl and whisk to combine.

3. In another bowl, combine grated zucchini, mashed banana, oil, maple syrup, vanilla extract, and egg, and whisk until well incorporated.

4. Fold wet ingredients into the dry ingredients until mixed through.

5. Place a spoonful of batter into each muffin cup.

6. Bake for 12–14 minutes, until muffins are cooked through.

7. Let cool and serve immediately or store in an airtight container for up to a week.

8. Freeze in an airtight container for up to a month.

Baby- and Toddler-Friendly Veggie Risotto

Makes 8–10 servings

I love any recipe where I can add in extra vegetables! Risotto is the perfect baby-friendly food example of how you can add just about any flavors you want and it will turn out delicious. This recipe is a favorite with my son for a healthy lunch or dinner!

Ingredients

5 cups chicken or veggie broth

1 tbsp. olive oil

¼ onion, finely chopped

1 cup carrot, grated

1 cup zucchini, grated

½ tbsp. kosher salt

½ tsp. black pepper

1½ cups arborio rice

½ cup Parmesan cheese, grated

Note: This recipe freezes well in individual portions for easy dinners or lunches any day of the week.

Directions

1. Add broth to a large saucepan and heat on low to warm through.

2. Heat olive oil and onion over medium heat and sauté for 2–3 minutes until onion is translucent.

3. Add carrot and zucchini, and season with salt and pepper.

4. Sauté the veggies for another 2–3 minutes.

5. Add rice and cook for 1 minute.

6. Add the warmed broth one cup at a time, stirring and allowing liquid to absorb before adding the next cup of broth. Continue until all of the broth is gone and rice is tender.

7. Add cheese and serve immediately.

Blackberry Yogurt Chia Teething Pops

Makes 24–28 one-ounce pops

When babies are teething, you will do anything to help ease their discomfort! My teething pops are the perfect snack—they not only taste delicious, but will also help soothe their tender gums.

Ingredients
2 cups plain yogurt

1 cup fresh blackberries

2 tbsp. chia seeds

Directions
1. Place all ingredients into a blender and process until smooth.
2. Pour the yogurt mixture into ice trays or small cups to create small popsicles.
3. Cut straws or popsicle sticks in half and insert in the middle of each pop before placing in the freezer.
4. Let the mixture freeze overnight, then pop out and store in a large plastic storage bag or container in the freezer for easy grab-snacks.

Roasted Root Vegetables with a Yogurt Tahini Dipping Sauce

Serves 6–8

Want to get your baby to eat veggies? These roasted veggies taste like candy and are even more delicious when drizzled or dipped into my yogurt tahini sauce. Make a batch at the beginning of the week and you have an easy and healthy snack for your baby whenever you need it!

Ingredients

4 carrots, peeled and diced

4 parsnips, peeled and diced

1 large beet, diced

2 cups butternut squash, diced

1 tbsp. avocado or olive oil

½ tsp. kosher or sea salt

¼ tsp. black pepper

1 tsp. fresh thyme leaves

For the Sauce

⅓ cup tahini

½ cup warm water

1 tsp. lemon juice

3 tbsp. plain yogurt

¼ tsp. kosher or sea salt

Directions

1. Preheat oven to 425 degrees.

2. Place all vegetables onto a parchment-lined baking sheet. Drizzle with oil and season with salt, pepper, and thyme.

3. Toss the vegetables with your hands to coat with seasoning.

4. Roast for 35–45 minutes, until vegetables are tender.

5. Meanwhile, combine tahini, water, lemon juice, yogurt, and salt and whisk until smooth. Set aside.

6. Serve the sauce over the vegetables or alongside for dipping. Store leftover sauce in the refrigerator for up to a week.

Note: This recipe is best eaten the day of or stored in the freezer the same day.

Mini Wild Salmon Patties with Lemon Dill Yogurt Sauce

Makes 4 patties

Salmon is high in omega-3s and is so good for your babe. My salmon patties with yogurt sauce are a delicious and cost-effective way to incorporate wild-caught salmon into your child's diet!

Ingredients

For the Salmon Patties

1 (15-oz.) can boneless and skinless wild-caught salmon

7 saltine crackers, finely crushed

1 egg

1 tbsp. lemon juice

¼ tsp. salt

¼ tsp. black pepper

1 tbsp. chives or finely diced scallion

For the Sauce

½ cup plain Greek yogurt

2 tbsp. lemon juice

1 tbsp. fresh dill

Pinch of salt (optional)

Directions

1. Preheat oven to 350 degrees.
2. Drain the liquid from the canned salmon and pick through the meat to ensure there are no bones or skin left behind.
3. Add salmon, crushed crackers, egg, lemon juice, salt, pepper, and chives to a large bowl.
4. With a fork, combine the salmon mixture until everything is well-incorporated.
5. Form small patties and place onto a parchment-lined baking sheet.
6. Bake for 20 minutes, until salmon patties are cooked though.
7. In the meantime, whisk together yogurt, lemon juice, dill, and salt until well combined.
8. Serve the patties alongside the yogurt sauce immediately.

Easy Broccoli Shells and Cheese

Serves 8

Every kid loves a comforting bowl of macaroni and cheese, and when it's homemade from real ingredients, you can feel good about your kids eating it! Broccoli adds extra nutrients to this kid favorite and makes this recipe a winner.

Ingredients

1 lb. pasta shells
1 cup fresh broccoli
   florets
2 tbsp. butter
2 tbsp. all-purpose flour
1½ cups whole milk
1 tsp. salt
½ tsp. black pepper
Pinch of nutmeg
1½ cups cheddar
   cheese, shredded
½ cup mozzarella
   cheese, shredded

Directions

1. Bring a large pot of water to a boil. Once water is boiling, salt the water and add the pasta.

2. Cook according to package directions until pasta is tender. Add broccoli to the boiling pasta water for the last 3–5 minutes of cooking to cook the broccoli.

3. As the pasta cooks, heat butter in a saucepan over medium heat.

4. Once the butter starts to melt, add the flour to the pan and whisk to combine.

5. Stir continuously for 2 minutes to allow flour and butter to cook a little.

6. Whisk in milk until thoroughly combined.

7. Season the béchamel sauce with salt, pepper, and nutmeg, and continue to stir until the sauce thickens and coats the back of a spoon, about 5–10 minutes.

8. Add shredded cheese to the béchamel sauce and turn off the heat. Stir the cheese until melted and set aside with the lid on.

9. Once the pasta and broccoli are done cooking, strain them in a colander.

10. Add the pasta and broccoli back to the large pasta pot and pour in the cheese sauce.

11. Stir to combine and serve immediately.

Mini Whole Wheat Vanilla Waffles

Makes 12 mini waffles

You would never know these waffles are good for you judging by their fluffy texture and delicious taste, but they're made with only the best ingredients—including an extra dose of protein due to my secret ingredient of cottage cheese, which your baby won't even detect! Make a batch and freeze for easy breakfasts any morning of the week.

Ingredients

1 cup whole wheat flour

1 cup all-purpose flour

1½ tbsp. baking powder

¼ tsp. salt

¼ cup cottage cheese

1 egg

½ cup melted coconut oil

1 tsp. pure vanilla extract

1½ cups milk (feel free to use almond or coconut milk here)

Directions

1. Combine both flours, baking powder, and salt in a large bowl.

2. In a smaller bowl, combine cottage cheese, egg, coconut oil, vanilla extract, and milk and whisk to combine thoroughly.

3. Slowly mix wet ingredients into the dry ingredients and whisk to combine. Use batter immediately.

4. Place 1–2 tablespoons of batter in the center of the waffle iron to create mini-size waffles.

5. Cook until done.

6. Serve with desired toppings.

Fun toppings: Any type of fruit, peanut butter, coconut shavings, maple syrup, and chia jam.

Mini Cheddar, Sweet Potato, and Leek Frittatas

Serves 12

Frittatas are a favorite in my house and I just love the mini versions even more! They are perfect for making in advance for easy breakfasts or healthy snacks full of protein for mama and baby. They freeze beautifully and are perfect for any day of the week.

Ingredients

1 tsp. coconut oil

1 cup sweet potato, finely diced

¼ cup leek, chopped

½ tsp. salt

½ tsp. black pepper

6 eggs

2 tbsp. milk

½ cup cheddar cheese, shredded

Directions

1. Preheat oven to 350 degrees.

2. Heat coconut oil over medium-high heat in a large skillet. Add diced sweet potato and leek to the pan, along with salt and pepper.

3. Cook for about 10 minutes, until sweet potatoes start to get tender, then let cool for about 5 minutes.

4. Meanwhile, beat eggs with milk, and add cheddar cheese.

5. Pour sweet potato and leek into the eggs and fold in gently.

6. Grease a mini muffin tin liberally and pour egg mixture into each cup until almost full.

7. Bake for 15–20 minutes, until eggs are cooked through.

8. Serve immediately or store in the freezer for easy breakfasts or snacks.

Bigger Bites

12+ months

At this stage in the game, I am willing to bet that your babe is a pro in the eating department, and for the most part is indulging in whatever mama's eating too! He or she has developed a taste for their favorite recipes and will definitely let you know when they don't like something. Don't be surprised if their favorite dish suddenly becomes something they turn their nose up at.

When babies reach the age of one year and above, they really start to form opinions about what they are eating and may decide to not eat something they used to love simply because of the color, or maybe now the texture is not appealing to them. Don't fret, however, because usually this stage is only temporary, and what I said in the Little Spoonfuls chapter still rings true—don't stop trying to feed that certain ingredient or recipe to them, because chances are next week they will be back to liking it again!

In this chapter, you will find recipes created specifically for the toddler stage and above. These recipes have become favorites of my son and I think your kiddos are going to love them too. I have incorporated some healthier snack options in this chapter as well because toddlers can be very hungry little people with their newfound ability to walk and move all over the place, and with that comes an increased appetite!

While some parents tend to get a little more relaxed in the nutrition department as their children get older, it is still just as important that they are eating healthy and whole foods that are good for their bodies. Kids will always like certain foods such as chicken nuggets, which is why in this chapter I give you healthier alternatives to some toddler favorites.

I have also included several recipes that we serve as a family meal (such as my butternut squash chili) because at this stage in the game, when babies are eating most of the same foods and meals that we are, it's nice to have some options that the whole family can eat as a meal as well!

Most importantly, I want to make sure that you have fun with your babes and the foods that they are eating!

Recipes

Note: Most recipes will make 4–6 servings, perfect for freezing or eating as a family.

Homemade Apple Fig Newtons

Makes 12–15 cookies

For the Dough

½ cup brown sugar (can
  sub coconut sugar)

½ cup coconut oil

1 egg

2 tsp. vanilla

1 tsp. orange juice

1 cup all-purpose flour

½ cup whole wheat flour

1 tbsp. ground flaxseed

½ tsp. orange zest

1 tsp. cinnamon

½ tsp. baking soda

½ tsp. salt

For the Filling

8 dried figs

1 apple, peeled and
  diced

1 oz. orange juice

½ cup water

For the Dough

1. Beat sugar and coconut oil until smooth.

2. Add in egg, vanilla, and orange juice, and continue to mix until smooth.

3. In another bowl, combine flours, flaxseed, orange zest, cinnamon, baking soda, and salt, and whisk to combine.

4. Slowly add dry ingredients into the wet ingredients while mixing at a low speed, until just combined.

5. Turn dough out on a floured surface and roll into a long, rectangular $\frac{1}{8}$-inch-thick piece of dough.

For the Filling

1. Combine figs, apple, orange juice, and water in a saucepan and bring to a boil.

2. Boil for 15 minutes until figs and apples are soft.

3. Place fig mixture into a food processor and blend until smooth. Let cool completely.

To Assemble

1. Preheat oven to 325 degrees.

continued on page 160

Tip: I like to roll this dough out onto parchment paper to make it easier to transfer onto a baking sheet.

2. Spread fig puree down the center of the dough, in a 1-inch strip.

3. Using a pastry scraper, fold up one side of the dough carefully, on top of the fig mixture. Repeat the same process on the other side of the dough, creating a log.

4. Place on a parchment-lined baking sheet and bake for 12–15 minutes, until dough is golden brown.

5. Let cool at least 5 minutes on a cooling rack and then slice into 1-inch cookies.

6. Store these cookies in the refrigerator for up to a week or freeze for up to a month.

Baked Gluten-Free Chicken Nuggets with Homemade Ketchup

Makes 20–24 nuggets

There's no need to buy frozen nuggets filled with unknown ingredients when you can make your own taste this good, and are actually made healthy for your toddler with wholesome ingredients!

For the Tenders

1 lb. chicken tenders (or use breasts and slice them yourself)

2 cups gluten-free crackers

½ cup gluten-free all-purpose flour

2 eggs, beaten

1 tsp. kosher or sea salt

½ tsp. black pepper

Avocado oil spray or olive oil spray

For the Ketchup

1 tsp. avocado oil

¼ cup onion, grated

1 clove garlic, minced

1 (15-oz.) can crushed tomatoes

1 tbsp. tomato paste

1 tbsp. Worcestershire sauce

1 tsp. molasses

½ tsp. kosher salt

¼ tsp. black pepper

For the Tenders

1. Preheat oven to 375 degrees.

2. Cut chicken into 1-inch bite-size nuggets.

3. Place crackers in a food processor and pulse until the crackers are the consistency of bread crumbs.

continued on page 163

4. Using wide bowls, place the flour, eggs, and ground crackers into 3 separate bowls.

5. Season the flour with salt and pepper.

6. For each nugget, lightly dust the chicken with flour to coat entirely. Dip the flour-coated chicken into the eggs and coat. Finally, dip the egg-coated chicken into the cracker crumbs and make sure it is coated.

7. Place nuggets on a wire rack on top of a baking sheet, and place into the oven.

8. Spray the nuggets with avocado oil spray and bake for 18–20 minutes.

9. Switch the oven to broil and broil for another 2 minutes to get a crispy crust.

For the Ketchup

1. Heat oil in a saucepan over medium heat.

2. Add onion and garlic and sauté for 2–3 minutes.

3. Add in crushed tomatoes, tomato paste, Worcestershire sauce, molasses, salt, and pepper, and whisk to combine.

4. Bring to a boil, and then reduce heat and let simmer for 30 minutes, until ketchup has thickened slightly.

5. Serve immediately or store in an airtight container in the refrigerator.

Healthy Toddler Tuna Salad Sammies

Makes 12 mini sandwiches

This tuna salad makes for an easy and healthy lunch for babies and toddlers, and it can all be prepped ahead of time to make your mom life easier!

Ingredients

1 can wild-caught tuna, drained (I prefer tuna in olive oil)

¼ cup Greek yogurt

2 tbsp. celery, grated

1 tsp. lemon juice

¼ tsp. kosher salt

¼ tsp. black pepper

¼ tsp. Old Bay Seasoning

1 egg

Whole wheat sprouted bread

1 cucumber, sliced

Directions

1. Mix all ingredients (except the bread and cucumber) together in a large bowl.

2. Cut out small circles of the bread with a cookie or biscuit cutter, and place a spoonful of tuna salad on one side. Place the other circle of bread on top to make a sandwich.

3. For mini cucumber sandwiches, slice the cucumber thin and place a teaspoon of tuna salad in between two slices.

4. Serve immediately.

Note: Tuna salad will store in the refrigerator for 2–3 days.

Tip: To make gluten-free, simply substitute gluten-free bread crumbs and flour in the recipe.

Baked Fish Sticks

Makes 10–12 sticks

Ingredients

1 lb. (about 16 oz.) cod or
   other white fish

1 cup all-purpose flour

1 tsp. salt

½ tsp. black pepper

2 cups panko bread crumbs

1 tbsp. fresh parsley, chopped

2 eggs

1 tbsp. olive oil or nonstick spray

Directions

1. Preheat oven to 400 degrees.

2. Cut cod into 1-inch strips.

3. Place flour on a plate and season with half of the salt and pepper.

4. On another plate, place the panko bread crumbs and season with the other half of the salt and pepper as well as the chopped parsley.

5. In a small bowl, add the eggs and whisk well until the yolks and whites are combined.

6. Take pieces of cod and lightly coat with flour and then place directly into the eggs and coat thoroughly. Shake off the excess egg, place into the bread crumbs, and coat well.

7. Place a baking rack onto a baking sheet, or line a baking sheet with parchment paper, and place fish sticks on top.

8. Drizzle with olive oil or nonstick spray and bake for 12 minutes, until fish is cooked through.

9. In the last minute of baking, turn the oven to broil to brown the fish.

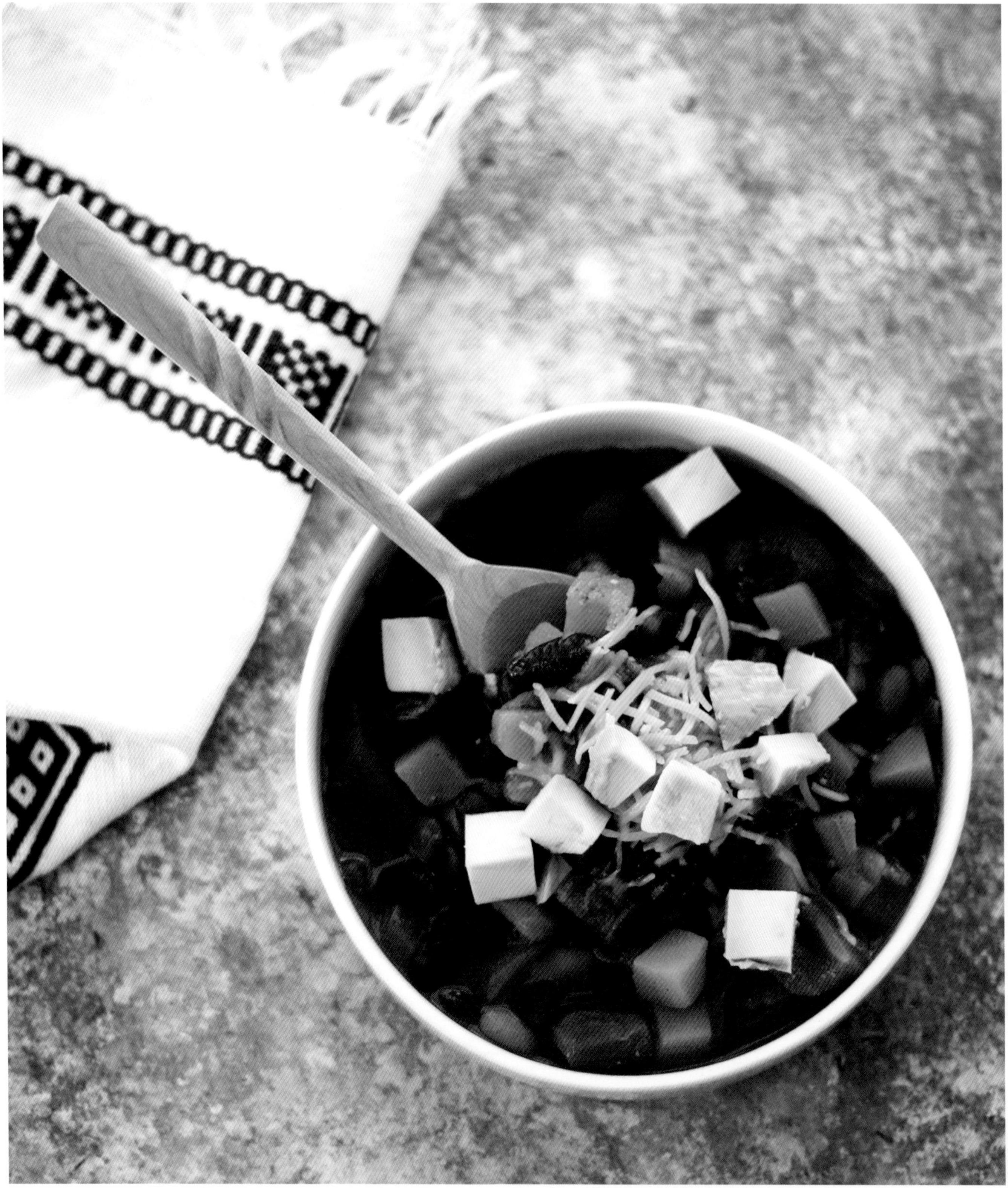

Kid-Friendly Butternut Squash Chili

Makes 12 toddler-size servings

Not only is this chili kid-friendly, but I can guarantee that your whole family will love it! Make a batch and freeze into portions if desired, or serve for a healthy vegetarian family dinner.

Ingredients

1 tbsp. avocado oil

1 cup onion, finely diced

1 tbsp. chili powder

1 tsp. cumin

1 tsp. paprika

1 tsp. garlic powder

1 tsp. onion powder

1 tbsp. nutritional yeast

1 (15-oz.) can diced tomatoes

1 (15-oz.) can kidney beans

1 (15-oz.) can pinto beans

1 (15-oz.) can black beans

1 cup butternut squash, diced

3 cups water

Shredded cheese, for topping (optional)

Avocado, for topping

1 tbsp. salt

1 tsp. or less black pepper

Directions

1. Heat oil in a large pot over medium heat.

2. Add in onion and sauté for 3 minutes or until onion is translucent.

3. Add chili powder, cumin, paprika, garlic powder, onion powder, and yeast to the onion, and cook the spices for two minutes.

4. Add can of tomatoes and season with salt and pepper.

5. Add in all beans, butternut squash cubes, and water, and bring to a boil.

6. Let simmer for 20 minutes until squash is tender, then serve with cheese and avocado.

Note: This chili freezes great and can be frozen into individual portions.

Fruit Spring Rolls

Makes 6 rolls

Toddlers are visual eaters, so I look for ways to make healthy ingredients fun and interesting for something new! These fruit spring rolls are so fun and you can get as creative as you want with them. I guarantee your kiddos will love dipping them into a tasty yogurt sauce for a healthy snack any time of day.

Ingredients

Warm water

6 spring roll sheets

1 kiwi

1 mango

¼ cup sliced strawberries

¼ cup blackberries

¼ cup blueberries

10–12 mint leaves

¼ cup sliced cucumber

½ cup plain yogurt

1 tsp. honey

1 tsp. lemon juice

Note: You can use any fruit and herb combinations that your family likes or is in season!

Directions

1. Fill a large, shallow dish with warm water.

2. Place the dried spring roll sheets into the water for 2–3 minutes, until they begin to soften.

3. Remove the softened spring roll sheets and shake off the excess water. Place on a clean surface and layer with fruit, mint leaves, and cucumber.

4. Carefully fold the bottom and top ends of the spring roll sheet up over the fruit and then roll the sides to create a burrito shape. Repeat until all rolls are done.

5. Mix yogurt, honey, and lemon juice in a small bowl.

6. Serve alongside the spring rolls as a dipping sauce.

Asian Chicken Meatballs with Coconut Rice

Makes 20–22 meatballs

These meatballs are perfect for tiny hands and are packed full of delicious flavor. This meal is not only kid-friendly, but doubles as a delicious and healthy family meal!

Ingredients

1 lb. ground chicken

1 tsp. low-sodium soy sauce

2 tbsp. + 1 tsp. hoisin sauce

1 tsp. fresh ginger, grated

1 tbsp. green onions, finely diced

1 egg

4 tbsp. panko bread crumbs

1 cup brown rice

3 cups full-fat coconut milk

2 tbsp. water

Directions

1. Preheat oven to 350 degrees.

2. Combine ground chicken, soy sauce, 1 teaspoon hoisin sauce, ginger, green onions, egg, and bread crumbs in a bowl and use a fork to combine all ingredients together.

3. Cook rice according to package directions, using coconut milk instead of water for the liquid.

4. Make 1-inch balls out of the ground chicken mixture and place on a parchment-lined baking sheet.

5. Bake for 20 minutes or until chicken is cooked through.

6. While the meatballs are cooking, heat 2 tablespoons hoisin sauce with 2 tablespoons water over low heat and whisk until the hoisin sauce has thinned out slightly.

7. When meatballs are finished cooking, toss them with the hoisin sauce and serve over coconut rice.

Mini Spinach and Cheese Ravioli with Homemade Marinara

I love a good shortcut in the kitchen, and wonton wrappers make homemade ravioli a breeze! Not only are these raviolis easy and made with simple ingredients, but they freeze beautifully too!

For the Ravioli

1 tsp. olive oil

1 garlic clove

2 cups frozen spinach, thawed

½ tsp. salt

⅛ tsp. black pepper

1 cup ricotta cheese

½ cup Parmesan cheese

1 egg

30 wonton wrappers

For the Marinara

1 tsp. olive oil

¼ cup onion, finely diced

1 garlic clove, minced

1 (15-oz.) can crushed tomatoes

1 tsp. Italian seasoning

1 tsp. salt

½ tsp. black pepper

For the Ravioli

1. Heat a skillet over medium heat and add the olive oil to the pan.
2. Add garlic and let simmer 1 minute until garlic becomes fragrant, and then add the spinach.
3. Sauté the spinach and garlic for 2–3 minutes and season with salt and pepper.

continued on next page

Spinach and Corn Quesadillas

Serves 1–2

Quesadillas are another great way to get your kiddos to eat their vegetables. They are easy to make and can be whipped up using whatever ingredients you have on hand. One of our favorite combinations is this recipe for my spinach and corn quesadillas!

Ingredients

1 tsp. olive oil

2 tbsp. red onion, finely diced

¼ cup corn kernels

¼ cup baby spinach, chopped

⅛ tsp. chili powder

⅛ tsp. black pepper

2 wheat tortillas

¼ cup cheddar cheese, shredded

Note: You can make extra quesadillas to freeze for easy, make-ahead meals!

Directions

1. Heat olive oil over medium heat, then add onion, corn, baby spinach, chili powder, and pepper, and sauté for 3–5 minutes until onion is translucent and spinach has wilted.

2. Remove from the pan and place one tortilla in the same pan.

3. Layer half the cheese onto the tortilla, then put the spinach and corn mixture on top of the first layer of cheese before layering the rest of the cheese.

4. Place the second tortilla on top and cook for about 3 minutes per side until the cheese has melted.

5. Cut into 4 pieces and serve immediately.

Spiced Black Beans, Kale, and Quinoa Bowls

Serves 6–8

These little bowls of goodness are packed full of nutrients for your babe and are perfect for meal prepping at the beginning of the week!

Ingredients

1 tbsp. olive oil

2 tbsp. onion, finely diced

1 cup kale, finely chopped

1 can black beans, drained and rinsed

1 tsp. salt

½ tsp. black pepper

1 tsp. cumin

½ tsp. chili powder

¾ cup quinoa, cooked

Directions

1. Heat olive oil over medium heat, and add diced onion and kale and sauté until kale is tender.

2. Add black beans to the pan along with salt, pepper, cumin, and chili powder, and cook for another 5 minutes, mashing the black beans slightly as they cook.

3. Combine the black bean and kale mixture with the quinoa, and fold together gently.

4. Serve immediately, or store in the fridge for up to a week.

Mini Chicken Pot Pies

Makes 12

These pot pies are super easy to make and are filled with lots of veggies and good protein for your little ones. They are perfect for tiny hands to pick up and enjoy!

Ingredients

1 tbsp. olive oil

3 boneless, skinless
   chicken thighs, diced (or
   1 breast)

1 tsp. salt

½ tsp. black pepper

½ cup leek, chopped

½ cup carrot, finely diced

½ cup potatoes, chopped
   and peeled

1 tsp. fresh thyme

1 garlic clove, finely
   minced

½ cup peas

2 tbsp. flour

½ cup whole milk

½ cup chicken stock

2 sheets puff pastry (thawed)

1 egg + 1 tsp. water

Directions

1. Preheat oven to 400 degrees.

2. Heat olive oil over medium heat and add the chicken, salt, and pepper.

3. Brown the chicken and then add leek, carrot, potatoes, thyme, and garlic.

4. Sauté for about 15 minutes, until veggies start to get tender. Add peas.

5. Add 2 tablespoons of flour and stir to coat the ingredients.

6. Pour in milk and chicken stock, and continue to cook until sauce starts to thicken, about 10 more minutes.

7. Slightly roll out the puff pastries onto a lightly floured surface.

8. Using two sizes of cookie cutters, cut out 12 larger circles for the bottom of the pot pies on one sheet of pastry, and then 12 slightly smaller circles of pastry on the second sheet. You will have to use some scraps to get the last two bottom circles.

continued on page 186

9. Grease a muffin tin lightly. Place the larger puff pastry circles in the bottom of each muffin.

10. Place a spoonful of the chicken pot pie filling on top of each pastry round.

11. Top with the smaller circle and press ends together with a fork.

12. Cut a slit in the top of each pot pie.

13. Whisk together egg and water and brush the tops of the pot pies lightly with the egg wash.

14. Bake for 15–17 minutes, until pastry is golden brown.

Note: This recipe freezes beautifully for easy make-ahead meals!

Beet Waffles
with Coconut Cinnamon Apples

Makes 8 waffles

Beets are a superfood for babies since they are packed with fiber and vitamin C, and they happen to be the most gorgeous color! I love adding them into different recipes for an instant vitamin boost. Your little one will love the pink hue and delicious taste of my healthy beet waffles!

Ingredients

1 cup whole wheat flour

½ cup all-purpose flour

2 tsp. baking powder

½ tsp. salt

1 tsp. cinnamon

½ cup Greek yogurt

½ cup Beet Applesauce (page 25)

1 egg

¾ cup buttermilk
  (or sub non-dairy here)

1 tsp. vanilla

For the Apples

1 tsp. coconut oil

1 apple, peeled and diced

1 tsp. cinnamon

1 tsp. maple syrup (optional)

Directions

1. Mix together both flours, baking powder, salt, and cinnamon in a large bowl.
2. In another bowl, combine the yogurt, Beet Applesauce, egg, buttermilk, and vanilla.

continued on page 189

3. Slowly fold the wet ingredients into the dry ingredients until well combined.

4. Heat a waffle iron and cook ¼ cup of batter at a time, setting aside each waffle as they finish cooking, until the batter is gone.

5. While the waffles cook, heat coconut oil over medium heat in a small saucepan.

6. Add the diced apple to the coconut oil along with the cinnamon.

7. Cook for 5–7 minutes, until the apple is tender.

8. Add maple syrup in the last couple minutes of cooking, if desired.

9. To serve, spoon some of the apple mix over the waffles.

Whole Wheat Cinnamon and Oat Muffins with Chocolate Chips

Makes 12 muffins

Muffins are such a great food to prep in advance on a weekly basis for easy snacking and breakfasts! This recipe is perfect for a healthy afternoon snack, or breakfast on the go for your baby or toddler.

Ingredients

¼ cup plain whole-milk yogurt (Greek or regular)

1 banana, mashed

¼ cup honey

¾ cup whole wheat flour

⅛ cup rolled oats

Pinch of salt

1 tsp. cinnamon

¼ cup mini dark chocolate chips (optional)

Directions

1. Preheat oven to 350 degrees.
2. Mix together yogurt, banana, and honey until well combined.
3. Add flour, oats, salt, and cinnamon to the bowl and stir until combined.
4. Pour batter into lined muffin tins and sprinkle with dark chocolate chips.
5. Bake for 20–25 minutes, until muffins are cooked through.
6. Serve warm or store in the refrigerator for up to a week or the freezer for up to a month.

Indian Tofu Bites with Yogurt Sauce

Serves 4

Indian flavors are a great way to expand your little one's taste buds and as long as you aren't adding heat, they usually will love it! These tofu bites are packed full of flavor and are so good for them, with spices like turmeric being used.

Ingredients

1 package firm tofu, drained and patted dry

1 tbsp. avocado oil

1 tsp. ground turmeric

1 tsp. cumin

½ tsp. salt

¼ tsp. black pepper

1 cup plain whole-milk Greek yogurt

1 tbsp. cucumber, peeled, seeded, and grated

1 tbsp. green onion, finely chopped

¼ tsp. coriander

½ tsp. cumin

1 tsp. lemon juice

Pinch of salt

Directions

1. Preheat oven to 350 degrees.

2. Thoroughly dry tofu by placing onto paper towels and pressing it gently to remove excess moisture.

3. Cut the tofu into 1-inch squares.

4. Combine oil, turmeric, cumin, salt, and pepper in a small bowl and stir to combine to make a paste.

5. Rub seasoning on all sides of the tofu evenly and place on a parchment-lined baking sheet.

6. Bake for 10 minutes, then flip tofu and bake on the other side for 10 more minutes.

7. While the tofu bakes, combine yogurt, cucumber, green onion, coriander, cumin, lemon juice, and salt in a small bowl and stir to combine. Set aside.

8. When tofu is done cooking, serve alongside the yogurt sauce for dipping.

Mini Baked Corn Dogs

Makes 16 corn dogs

My healthier take on a corn dog will have you feeling good about what your toddler is eating, and I can guarantee that they will gobble them up without hesitation!

Ingredients

1 cup corn bread dry mix

1 tsp. chili powder

½ tsp. black pepper

1 egg

½ cup milk

3 tbsp. olive oil

8 organic turkey or beef hot dogs

Directions

1. Preheat oven to 425 degrees.

2. Add dry corn bread mix, chili powder, and black pepper to a large bowl and whisk to combine.

3. In a separate bowl, beat egg, and add milk and oil.

4. Add wet ingredients into the dry ingredients and stir to combine (mixture should be thick).

5. Cut hot dogs in half and skewer with wooden skewers or popsicle sticks.

6. Take a paper towel and pat the hot dogs to remove excess moisture, so the cornbread mix will be able to stick.

7. Using a knife, spread the cornbread mix on all sides of the hot dog until coated.

8. Place the mini corn dogs on a parchment-lined baking sheet and bake for 12 minutes or until golden brown.

9. Serve with ketchup or mustard.

Muffin Tin Mini Turkey Meatloaf

Serves 8

Everything is more fun in mini form, and my muffin tin turkey meatloaves make for perfectly portioned servings for your little one! You will love this tiny version of a classic recipe.

Ingredients

1 tbsp. olive oil

½ cup onion, finely diced

1 garlic clove, finely minced

1 tsp. kosher salt

½ tsp. black pepper

1 lb. ground turkey

1 egg

½ cup bread crumbs

¼ cup milk

1 tbsp. Italian seasoning

2 tsp. ketchup + more for topping

Directions

1. Preheat oven to 350 degrees.

2. Heat olive oil in a pan over medium heat and add chopped onion and garlic.

3. Sauté for 2–3 minutes, until onion is translucent.

4. Remove the onion and garlic from the heat and let cool slightly.

5. Combine all ingredients in a large bowl, including the cooked onion and garlic, and stir with a wooden spoon until just combined.

6. Spoon ¼ cup of meatloaf mixture into a greased muffin tin until full.

7. Spoon a teaspoon of ketchup over each meatloaf muffin and spread to cover the top.

8. Bake for 25 minutes or until meatloaf is cooked through.

9. Serve immediately or freeze in individual portions for a later date.

Strawberry Kiwi Fruit Leather

Serves 12

There is no need to buy fruit snacks that are full of refined sugars when you can make your own at home this easily. These strawberry kiwi fruit leather roll-ups are perfect for your toddler's snack time!

Ingredients

3 cups strawberries, hulled and diced

3 kiwis, peeled and diced

3 tbsp. honey (for babies over 1 year) or agave nectar if necessary for sweetness

1 tbsp. water

Directions

1. Place all ingredients into a large saucepan and heat over medium heat.

2. Cook for 15–20 minutes until fruit has reduced and sauce has thickened.

3. Using an immersion blender, puree the fruit mixture. Alternatively, place into a food processor or blender and process until smooth.

4. Preheat oven to 170 degrees or as low as your oven will go.

5. Spread the fruit onto a silpat or parchment-lined baking sheet into an even and very thin layer.

6. Bake for 3–4 hours until fruit is dry.

7. Cut into strips and roll up in wax paper to store for up to a week.

Taking Care of You—Mamas Only

As moms, we tend to forget about ourselves and put everyone else first. With that can come letting our health slide, and that isn't good for anyone! I am a firm believer that if you put good things into your body, then you will feel better and will have a higher energy level, which we all need as mamas!

For me, it's all about what's easy—if I have healthy items available that are a cinch to whip up, then I can stop myself from eating something not so good for me. On top of that, if I am honest with myself, half the time my breakfast or lunch (or both) are eaten standing up and in stages because I'm always chasing around an active toddler! Having low energy is never a good thing with babies, who don't care if you are tired or not! So why not give your body the fuel it needs to be the best you?

My day usually consists of sharing a smoothie in the morning with Parks, and then I have some version of a nourish bowl or sandwich for lunch, and I've got to have a few healthy snacks that keep my blood sugar stable throughout the day (and it doesn't hurt if they curb my sweet tooth too!).

I put together a few of my favorite recipes that I make for myself on the regular! These recipes are easy to make during all the chaos of this thing called parenthood, and I promise you will feel so much better when you take the time to take care of yourself.

Recipes

Nourish Bowl

Serves 1

I *love* these bowls full of goodness! At the beginning of each week, I make a batch of grains, boil some eggs, and then I have a 5-minute healthy lunch ready whenever I am! I just add the egg and other ingredients right before eating.

Ingredients

2 eggs (these will be soft boiled or fried)

½ cup cooked farro (or other whole grain)

1 cup baby spinach

½ cup chickpeas or cannellini beans

1 tbsp. avocado or olive oil

1 tbsp. lemon juice

1 tsp. kosher salt

½ tsp. black pepper

Directions

1. Fry or boil eggs to desired doneness.

2. Combine farro, spinach, eggs, and beans in a bowl.

3. Mix oil, lemon juice, salt, and pepper separately in a small bowl.

4. Drizzle the vinaigrette over top of the nourish bowl and serve immediately.

Note: Each of these ingredients can be prepped at the beginning of the week so you can have lunch all week long!

Cherry Mocha Latte Power Smoothie

Makes 1 generous serving

A smoothie that has it all, including coffee . . . because caffeine.

Ingredients
1 cup fresh spinach

¼ cup frozen or fresh dark cherries

½ cup cooled or chilled coffee

1 tbsp. cocoa powder

1 tbsp. hemp seeds

1 tbsp. chia seeds

1 tbsp. flaxseed

¼ cup rolled oats

½ frozen banana

1 tsp. turmeric (fresh or ground)

Directions
1. Place all ingredients into a blender and process until smooth.
2. Take a moment and breathe, and drink your smoothie.

Note: To make this a lactation smoothie, add in brewer's yeast and feel free to omit coffee or use decaf.

Mango Coconut Granola

Makes 4–5 cups

I love making a large batch of homemade granola at the beginning of each week. It's great for a snack, sprinkled on yogurt, or with milk poured on top. If I have healthy snacks prepped, then I am setting myself up for success!

Ingredients

4 cups rolled oats

½ cup toasted almonds, sliced or chopped

¼ cup walnuts, macadamia nuts, or nut of choice

½ cup coconut, shredded

2 tbsp. ground flaxseed

2 tbsp. brewer's yeast (optional; good for breastfeeding mamas)

2 tbsp. wheat germ

½ cup honey

½ cup melted coconut oil

1 tsp. vanilla

¼ cup dried mango, chopped

Directions

1. Preheat oven to 300 degrees.

2. Combine oats, nuts, ¼ cup of shredded coconut, flaxseed, brewer's yeast, and wheat germ in a large bowl, and stir to combine.

3. Melt honey and coconut oil together and then stir in vanilla.

4. Pour over oat mixture until all the granola is coated.

5. Spread evenly onto a parchment-lined baking sheet and bake for 20–30 minutes, until golden brown.

6. Let cool and add the dried mango and the rest of the coconut.

Note: Cookies will store in an airtight container for up to a week. You can also freeze the dough in already scooped portions for easy baking!

Everything but the Kitchen Sink Lactation Cookies

Makes 24 cookies

These cookies are great to have on hand if you are breastfeeding; they'll help amp up that milk supply and keep your energy level high! They are healthy with a little added sweetness, because we deserve a little treat every now and then. If you aren't breastfeeding, simply omit the brewer's yeast and you still have a delicious sweet treat for yourself!

Ingredients

½ cup unsalted butter, room temperature

1 cup brown sugar or coconut sugar

1 egg

1 tsp. vanilla

2 tbsp. almond butter

3 cups rolled oats

1½ cups all-purpose flour

2 tbsp. ground flaxseed

3–5 tbsp. brewer's yeast

1 tsp. baking soda

1 tsp. cinnamon

½ tsp. salt

¼ cup chocolate chips

¼ cup toffee pieces or nuts of your choice

¼ cup mini M&Ms

Directions

1. Preheat oven to 350 degrees.

2. Cream together butter and sugar with an electric mixer until smooth and fluffy.

3. Add in egg and beat until smooth.

4. Mix in vanilla and almond butter.

5. In a large bowl, combine oats, flour, flaxseed, yeast, baking soda, cinnamon, and salt and whisk to combine.

6. Slowly incorporate the dry ingredients into the wet ingredients until just combined.

7. Stir in chocolate chips, toffee pieces, and M&Ms.

8. Scoop equally sized balls, about 1 inch each, and place onto a parchment-lined baking sheet.

9. Press the cookies slightly on top and bake for 10–12 minutes.

Avocado Green Goddess Sandwich

Serves 1

I love this easy sandwich that is an amped-up version of my favorite avocado toast! It's a mixture of whole grains, healthy fats, and protein, which will keep you going through the lunch hour slump!

Ingredients

Sprouted whole grain bread

2 tbsp. hummus

6 slices of cucumber

¼ cup baby kale or spinach

¼ avocado, sliced

Organic turkey or chicken
   lunch meat (optional)

Salt and pepper, to taste

Directions

1. Toast bread.

2. Spread both pieces of bread with hummus, and then layer the rest of the ingredients on top, ending with avocado.

3. Season with salt and pepper (and chili flakes if you dare!).

4. Serve immediately.

Healthy Almond Butter and Coconut Bars

Makes 12 bars

These bars are perfect to make on a Sunday and store in the freezer for when that afternoon sweet tooth or snack attack hits. They are full of protein and taste amazing! These bars are one of my all-time favorite snacks!

Ingredients

8 medjool dates

2 cups rolled oats

1 cup almond butter

½ cup coconut oil, melted

½ cup honey

Pinch of salt

¼ cup coconut, shredded

1 tbsp. chia seeds

¼ cup whey protein powder (optional)

Note: Bars are best kept chilled until ready to eat in order for them not to get too soft.

Directions

1. Soak dates in water for 15 minutes. Remove the pits.

2. Pulse oats in a food processor until ground like flour.

3. Add almond butter, coconut oil, honey, dates, salt, shredded coconut, chia seeds, and whey protein.

4. Pulse to combine all ingredients until the mixture starts to stick together.

5. Press the mixture onto a parchment-lined baking sheet in one single layer.

6. Place the pressed mixture into the freezer for thirty minutes.

7. Slice into squares and store in baggies in the freezer for easy-grab snacks.

Asian Chicken Salad with a Spicy Peanut Vinaigrette

By taking a few shortcuts with this salad, you can have a restaurant-quality salad ready to eat at any given time! I love prepping some of these ingredients in advance so I can give my body something that will nourish it and give me the energy I need to keep up with a toddler.

For the Vinaigrette

2 tbsp. creamy peanut butter

1 tsp. soy sauce

1 tsp. fresh ginger, grated and peeled

⅛–¼ cup water

1 tsp. chili sesame oil (substitute regular sesame oil if you don't want it spicy)

1 tsp. rice wine vinegar

For the Salad

1 cup pre-packaged slaw mix

¼ cup edamame, shelled

¼ cup peanuts (can substitute cashews or omit altogether if desired)

1 green onion, sliced

½ cup shredded rotisserie chicken (this just makes it extra-easy—feel free to cook your own chicken breasts!)

Directions

1. Heat peanut butter, soy sauce, ginger, and ¼ cup of water in a small saucepan over medium heat, and whisk until smooth. Add the other ¼ cup of water if needed for consistency.

2. Remove from heat, and whisk in the oil and rice wine vinegar to finish the vinaigrette. Set aside or chill in the refrigerator (it will store for two weeks).

3. To assemble the salad, mix slaw with edamame, peanuts, and green onion, and top with chicken.

4. Drizzle desired amount of dressing over salad and serve immediately.

Two-Minute Homemade Seasoned Popcorn

Serves 1 well-deserving mama

I am a sucker for a salty snack and ever since I learned how to make my own individual portions of freshly popped popcorn at home, I have been hooked! You can buy un-popped kernels in a jar at most supermarkets. Making your own microwaved popcorn with loose kernels and brown paper lunch bags may be the best trick ever. It's cost-effective, healthy, and you can season it differently every day—it doesn't get better than that!

Ingredients
⅓ cup popcorn kernels
Brown paper lunch bag

Toppings
1 tbsp. melted grass-fed
    butter or ghee
Parmesan cheese
Black pepper
Kosher salt
Nutritional yeast
Curry powder
Cajun seasoning

Directions
1. Place popcorn in the brown paper bag and fold over twice to seal the bag.

2. Microwave for 2 minutes until kernels have popped.

3. Pour melted butter over the top of the popcorn, sprinkle with desired seasonings, shake in the bag, and enjoy a healthy and satisfying snack!

Note: Any of your favorite seasonings will do here!

Bagel and Lox Sandwiches with Herbed Cream Cheese

Serves 1

This is a recipe that I love for an easy breakfast or lunch. I prep the cream cheese in advance and store it in the refrigerator so it's ready whenever I am! It's slightly decadent, giving me just the mommy-break I need every now and then.

Ingredients

8 oz. cream cheese, room temperature

2 tbsp. chives, chopped

2 tbsp. fresh dill, chopped

1 clove garlic, minced

½ tsp. salt

¼ tsp. black pepper

Everything bagel

Smoked salmon

Directions

1. Combine cream cheese, chives, dill, garlic, salt, and pepper in a bowl and stir until combined (or use a stand mixer to combine).

2. Toast the bagel and spread a layer of cream cheese on both sides.

3. Place a couple pieces of smoked salmon on the bottom half of the bagel and place the top half back on.

4. Cut in half and serve immediately.

Clean and Green Juice

Serves 1

This juice is full of ingredients that are great for detoxing and are immune-boosting as well. It's a refreshing way to start your day or simply to add to your regular diet to ensure you are getting some serious vitamins! You can blend it or juice it, but either way you will love how refreshing and healthy this drink really is!

Ingredients

½ lemon

1-inch piece fresh ginger

2 cups spinach

½ apple

1 celery stalk

½ cucumber

2 tbsp. fresh parsley

Coconut water (not needed if you have a juicer)

Note: Juice is best if consumed within 24 hours of making.

Directions

For a Juice Machine

1. Place all ingredients, skin and all, into the juicer one at a time, according to the manufacturer's instructions, until the juice is released from the machine. (You will not need coconut water.)

2. Serve immediately over ice.

For a Blender

1. Peel the lemon and the ginger, and de-seed the lemon.

2. Place all ingredients into the blender, including the coconut water.

3. Blend on High until all ingredients are smooth.

4. Strain the smoothie to remove pulp if desired, or serve as is.

5. Pour over ice as desired and serve immediately.

Buckeye Energy Balls

Makes 18–20

Chocolate and peanut butter are one of those epic combinations that everyone loves. These remind me of a dessert truffle that I love called buckeyes, but without all the bad fats and sugar. These balls satisfy my sweet tooth and keep me going through the late afternoon since they are filled with protein and oats!

Ingredients

2 cups rolled oats

½ cup creamy peanut butter

¼ cup coconut oil, melted

10 dates

3 tbsp. honey

2 tbsp. chia seeds

2 tbsp. protein powder

2 tbsp. wheat germ

¼ cup dark chocolate chips

Directions

1. Pulse oats in a food processor until they are a flourlike consistency.

2. Add peanut butter, coconut oil, dates, honey, chia seeds, protein powder, and wheat germ, and process until the mixture starts to come together.

3. Stir in chocolate chips.

4. Form 1-inch round balls and place into the freezer for 30 minutes before eating, or refrigerate.

Note: Buckeye balls are best stored in the refrigerator until ready to eat.

Acknowledgments

To my sweet baby boy, Parks, who made me fall in love and have a passion for creating recipes for all the kiddos out there. Your hearty appetite and enthusiasm for trying new flavors challenges me to keep creating new recipes every day. I wouldn't have created this book had you not come into my life and changed it forever for the better. Mama loves you more than you know, little sweet potato.

To my husband, Canean, who is forever supportive of me and my creative endeavors. You are my biggest fan, my encouragement, and you love me through all of my crazy. Thanks for allowing me to have days where I probably wasn't the best wife, didn't shower, and made you eat baby food for dinner. I love you forever and always, and am so glad I get to do this life with you. Thank you for giving me our son, who is no doubt our greatest accomplishment! I love you as big as the beach!

To my mom, who let me cook with her when I was little and made me fall in love with being in the kitchen at an early age. Thank you for teaching me about healthy food and giving me the opportunity to appreciate food that is good for me. I love you for it, and for being such an amazing mom that answers her phone 100 times a day . . . what would I do without you?

To my editor, Leah, who saw something in me before I saw it in myself, and took a chance on me. I am forever grateful for our paths crossing and for your guidance through two cookbooks. Thank you for the creative freedom and for the amazing feedback through the whole process. You made a dream come true for me and that I will always be thankful for. Cheers to this just being the beginning of our journey together.

To my readers and my fellow mommies, thank you for taking time to read what I write and for inspiring me on a daily basis. You are the reason I get to have the best job I could have ever dreamed of, and I love you so much for it! XO

Conversion Charts

METRIC AND IMPERIAL CONVERSIONS
(These conversions are rounded for convenience)

Ingredient	Cups/Tablespoons/Teaspoons	Ounces	Grams/Milliliters
Butter	1 cup/ 16 tablespoons/ 2 sticks	8 ounces	230 grams
Cheese, shredded	1 cup	4 ounces	110 grams
Cream cheese	1 tablespoon	0.5 ounce	14.5 grams
Cornstarch	1 tablespoon	0.3 ounce	8 grams
Flour, all-purpose	1 cup/1 tablespoon	4.5 ounces/0.3 ounce	125 grams/8 grams
Flour, whole wheat	1 cup	4 ounces	120 grams
Fruit, dried	1 cup	4 ounces	120 grams
Fruits or veggies, chopped	1 cup	5 to 7 ounces	145 to 200 grams
Fruits or veggies, puréed	1 cup	8.5 ounces	245 grams
Honey, maple syrup, or corn syrup	1 tablespoon	.75 ounce	20 grams
Liquids: cream, milk, water, or juice	1 cup	8 fluid ounces	240 milliliters
Oats	1 cup	5.5 ounces	150 grams
Salt	1 teaspoon	0.2 ounce	6 grams
Spices: cinnamon, cloves, ginger, or nutmeg (ground)	1 teaspoon	0.2 ounce	5 milliliters
Sugar, brown, firmly packed	1 cup	7 ounces	200 grams
Sugar, white	1 cup/1 tablespoon	7 ounces/0.5 ounce	200 grams/12.5 grams
Vanilla extract	1 teaspoon	0.2 ounce	4 grams

OVEN TEMPERATURES

Fahrenheit	Celsius	Gas Mark
225°	110°	¼
250°	120°	½
275°	140°	1
300°	150°	2
325°	160°	3
350°	180°	4
375°	190°	5
400°	200°	6
425°	220°	7
450°	230°	8

Index